STAGE MANAGING
and
THEATRE ETIQUETTE

Stage Managing and Theatre Etiquette

⊷❲ A BASIC GUIDE ❳⊶

Linda Apperson

IVAN R. DEE
Chicago

Library of Congress Cataloging-in-Publication Data:
    Apperson, Linda, 1950–
    Stage managing and theatre etiquette : a basic guide / Linda Apperson.
        p.   cm.
    Includes index.
    ISBN: 978-1-56663-201-0
    (pbk. : alk. paper)
        1. Stage management.   I. Title.
    PN2085.A66   1998   98-20546
    792'.023—dc21

For Clyde and Jessica

Contents

Acknowledgments   7
Prologue   9

1. Pre-production   15
   Before Rehearsals Begin   16
   Plots and Ground Plan   17
   Rehearsal Props   21
   Who's Who in the Production   24

2. Rehearsals   34
   Building the Prompt Book   35
   Information Hub   38
   Timing   42
   Tech Rehearsals   43
   Set Changes   45
   Notes   49
   Speeches   51

3. Performance   56
   Calling the Show   57
   Timing   61
   Details   63

4. Authority   69

5. Safety   74

6. Variations on the Job   78

7. Challenges of Theatre Life   83

8. Other Theatre Jobs   86
   Props   86
   Costumes   89
   Acting   90
   Lights   91
   Other Essential Jobs   92

Appendices
   I. Glossary   94
   II. Supplies   99
   III. Miscellaneous Tips   101
   IV. Callboard   104
   V. Sample Shift Plot   109
   VI. Sample Prop Plot   112
   VII. Sample Prompt Script Pages   114

Index   119

Acknowledgments

FOR seeing me through my early years as a stage manager, I want to thank Tony Mendez, David Rovine, John Davin, Bridgett Bartlett, Patti Haine, and Nelson Huber. Thanks also to Jacqueline Wender, Kathryn Green, Patrick McKenna, Mike Ramsaur, and Diana Bonet for reviewing the early drafts of this book. And special thanks to all the extraordinary people with whom I have had the privilege to create theatre and who have enriched my life in countless ways.

Prologue

THIS book is for people new to theatre or to stage managing. Perhaps you have always wanted to do theatre but have never tried. Perhaps you are involved in your first school play and want to learn more about stage managing. Or maybe you are in college, trying to find a direction for your theatrical energies. If stage managing intrigues you, this book can help you learn what managing the stage is all about.

Of course, reading cannot replace doing. The best way to learn to stage manage is to stage manage. But a few guidelines will help. I am writing this book to share my own experiences and hard-earned lessons.

I made my theatrical debut when I was twelve, in the chorus of *H.M.S. Pinafore*. The following year I sang Katisha in *The Mikado*. A talented, ambitious, elementary school music teacher directed both productions and, without either of us realizing it, taught me almost everything I needed to know to be a successful stage manager. I learned the gratification of a job well done, the joy of giving pleasure to others through performing, and the effort needed to accomplish those things. I also learned self-discipline and self-control. We had to be at rehearsal on time, know our material when we got there, and maintain silence unless we were actually singing. (If seventy eleven- and twelve-year-olds can be quiet while others are working on their parts, anyone can.)

We practiced strict performance decorum. We were not to draw attention to ourselves but blend in with the group to be part of a larger whole. We were expected to stand up straight, watch the director (not each other or the audience), and concentrate on what we were doing. We were to sing out and do our very best every time. As a result, we created powerful, beautiful music. And I got hooked on musical theatre. Over the years I applied all the lessons I learned in school choir to my backstage work.

I took a long time to discover stage managing. As a theatre major in college, I knew that I wanted to do theatre and that I didn't want to act. I worked on prop crews, and eventually a professor asked me to assistant stage manage. No training was available, and I wasn't sure what a stage manager did, but I stumbled my way through two productions. I called "places" and light cues and took notes in rehearsal and did whatever the director told me to do, but I did not begin to understand the job. (I could have used this book then.) I did not see the light until I dropped out of college and went to work in a dinner theatre. I learned there that the stage manager did all the things I liked to do and was already good at: organize, plan, and analyze and dispense information. I had found my niche.

I earned my living in theatre as a stage manager for twelve years. In that time I managed more than ninety productions—over three thousand performances. I felt blessed to do what for me was essentially playing for a living. And I got paid for it!

I have worked at various positions, from props,

wardrobe, dresser, and light operator to stints in the box office and house managing. I have also done some acting. But the job I do best and love most is managing the stage. The discipline I learned so many years earlier in school choir advanced my career in theatre arts and increased the enjoyment I derived from my work. I was extremely lucky to have a gifted music teacher to introduce me to the basic rules of performance etiquette. I would like to share what I have learned using those guidelines, and to thank Mrs. Pipho for teaching me my craft.

Regarding the quotes that appear in italic after some chapter titles and subheadings: While searching the Stanford University library, I chanced upon a book entitled *A Short Account of the Amateur Dramatic Club of St. Bartholomew's Hospital* by Stephen Townsend, published in London in 1888. I checked it out of the library immediately, and as I read it I was struck by two things. First, Mr. Townsend's writing style and choice of words are simply delightful, and second, almost everything he wrote more than a hundred years ago still applies. The primary change since then is in job titles. As described in his book, in 1888 the stage manager also functioned as director; after the show opened, the prompter (and call boy) carried out most of the responsibilities of the modern-day stage manager. But the structure of the job and the challenges associated with it are remarkably similar. I have taken the liberty of including quotes from Mr. Townsend's text as a counterpoint to my own opinions about what makes a good stage manager.

STAGE MANAGING
and
THEATRE ETIQUETTE

⁘[1]⁘

Pre-production

*[The holder of this office should always aim at
the highest, though he may never attain it. He
should spare himself no trouble, think no detail beneath his consideration, no minutiae
unworthy of attention. All this he should do
for the sake of the art of which, although an
amateur, he professes to be a student; for, if he
hopes to meet with gratitude from his colleagues, or an appreciation from his audience,
proportionate to the extent of his labours, he
will be doomed to inevitable chagrin and dis-
appointment.]*

THE stage manager is responsible for making sure everything relating to a particular production happens when and
how it is supposed to happen, and conveying all pertinent
information about time and place to all parties involved. In
the course of the play, any time there are changes in time
and/or place between scenes or acts, a stage manager over-

sees the alterations that will show the audience that change. In order to accomplish this, the stage manager must know virtually everything there is to know about the show. He or she must have a concrete vision of what the show should be according to its various directors and designers, and make this vision reality. To quote an unknown sage, "It's a dirty job, but somebody's got to do it."

So what exactly does a stage manager do?

Before Rehearsals Begin

1. Read the script and do scene plots. Write out where each scene takes place and who is in it. You may also be responsible for rehearsal props; if so, add props needed to this list. Don't include costumes (actors track their own costume changes—at least, one hopes they know what they are supposed to wear), but you should be aware of any quick changes or costumes used as props or preset—that is, on the set at the start of the scene, not brought on by the actors.

2. Get the ground plan from the designer or technical director and tape an outline, using the actual dimensions of the set, on the rehearsal room floor to indicate walls, doors, stairs, and platforms. You can use different colors to indicate different settings within the same show (for example, green for Act 1, red for Act 2).

3. Gather rehearsal props and set pieces. Use only hand props in rehearsal: the objects actors actually carry or touch. Likewise, the only set pieces you should use are representations of furniture (for example, two folding chairs to make a sofa).

4. Compile a list of names, addresses, and business and

home phone numbers for everyone involved in the production and distribute copies to everyone.

5. Make sure everyone involved knows when and where the first and subsequent rehearsals are taking place.

6. Print out as much of a rehearsal schedule as is available and make copies for cast members, directors, and designers.

7. Meet everyone—get to know your company.

Plots and Ground Plan

Create a master plan during the rehearsal process to help you in making the vision of the production real. This plan will enable you to run the rehearsals and the show. You should know the show as well as possible before rehearsals begin. Read the play two or three times before the first audition, rehearsal, or production meeting. Do rough prop, set, and costume plots to learn the details. The plots list each piece of these items in the production and where it is located, broken down by scene. These will change as rehearsals progress. (If you have a computer, the plots, company address list, and rehearsal schedule can be stored on it and easily accessed for updating.)

The following charts are rehearsal worksheets for *Fiddler on the Roof.* The first one is a scene-by-scene breakdown. It includes only the props that are actually touched by the cast. You are likely to be writing this before you see the set designs (props and set pieces indicated in scripts are frequently taken from the original Broadway production), so keep in mind that this is a skeleton chart and is subject to change.

The second chart is a detailed view of what characters

When	Where	What	Who
Act 1 Prologue	Tevye's house—exterior		Fiddler, Tevye, Villagers, Golde, Yente, Avram, Nahum, Lazar Wolf, Mendel, Rabbi
sc 1	Tevye's house—interior	kitchen: table and chairs, logs basket, book, basket w/potatoes, mop and bucket	Golde, Tzeitel, Hodel, Shprintze, Bielke, Chava, Yente, Motel
sc 2	Tevye's house—exterior	cart with cheeses and milk pails, newspaper	Tevye, Golde, Mordcha, Mendel, Perchik, Avram, Villagers
sc 3	Tevye's house—interior	table, candles, matches	Golde, Tevye, Tzeitel, Hodel, Chava, Shprintze, Bielke, Motel
sc 4	Inn	tables and chairs, bar, bottles, glasses	Avram, Lazar Wolf, Mendel, Village men, Mordcha, Fyedka, Russians, Tevye
sc 5	street—outside inn		Fiddler, Lazar Wolf, Tevye, Village men, Russians, Constable
sc 6	Tevye's house—exterior	bench, pump or well, potatoes, peeler, pan, pails, bucket	Perchik, Hodel, Shprintze, Bielke, Golde, Tevye, Tzeitel, Chava, Motel
sc 7	Tevye's bedroom	bed, lamp	Golde, Tevye, Villagers, Rabbi, musicians, Grandma Tzeitel, Frumah-Sarah
sc 8	Motel's tailor shop	table, book, Motel's wedding hat	Motel, Chava, Villagers, Mordcha, Avram, Shandel, Fyedka, Sasha, Russian
sc 9	Tevye's house—exterior	wedding canopy, candles, wine goblet (to be crushed)	Tzeitel, Tevye, Golde, Hodel, Chava, Bielke, Shprintze, Motel, Villagers, Rabbi

Scene	Location	Props/Set	Characters
sc 10	Tevye's house—exterior	divider, tables and chairs on each side, tables with wedding gifts: include pillows, candlesticks (one breaks)	Mordcha, Villagers, Rabbi, Mendel, Golde, Tevye, Tzeitel, Motel, Hodel, Chava, Bielke, Shprintze, Yente, Shandel, Perchik, Avram, Constable, Russians
Act 2 Prologue	Tevye's house—exterior	bench	Tevye
sc 1	Tevye's house—exterior		Hodel, Perchik, Tevye, Golde
sc 2	Village street		Yente, Tzeitel, Villagers, Mendel, Rabbi, Avram
sc 3	railroad station	bench, suitcase	Hodel, Tevye
sc 4	Village street		Villagers, Avram, Mordcha, Rabbi, Mendel, Shandel
sc 5	Motel's tailor shop	table, sewing machine, sewn fabric, shirt	Villagers, Motel, Tzeitel, Avram, Rabbi, Golde, Fyedka, Chava, Tevye, Shprintze, Bielke
sc 6	a road	cart	Tevye, Golde, Chava, Villagers
sc 7	Tevye's barn		Yente, 2 boys, Golde, Lazar Wolf, Avram, Mendel, Mordcha, Villagers, Tevye, Constable, 2 Russians
sc 8	Tevye's house—exterior	cart, bundles, suitcases, pots and pans, silver goblets, cloth, books, doll in blanket, trunk, rope	Motel, Tzeitel, Shprintze, Bielke, Golde, Yente, Tevye, Lazar Wolf, Chava, Fyedka, Fiddler

	1 P	1-1	1-2	1-3	1-4	1-5	1-6	1-7	1-8	1-9	1-10	2 P	2-1	2-2	2-3	2-4	2-5	2-6	2-7	2-8
Fiddler	×				×	×	×	×		×	×	×	×		×				×	×
Tevye	×		×	×	×	×	×	×	×	×	×	×					×	×	×	×
Villagers	×		×	×	×	×		×		×	×		×	×		×	×	×	×	
Golde	×	×	×	×			×		×	×	×						×	×	×	×
Yente	×	×									×			×			×		×	×
Avram	×		×		×				×					×		×	×		×	
Nahum	×																			
Lazar Wolf	×				×	×								×					×	×
Mendel	×		×		×					×	×			×		×	×		×	
Rabbi	×							×		×	×			×		×	×			×
Tzeitel		×		×			×			×	×									×
Hodel		×		×			×			×	×		×		×					×
Chava		×		×			×		×	×	×						×	×		×
Shprintze		×		×			×			×	×						×			×
Bielke		×		×			×			×	×						×			×
Motel		×		×	×		×		×	×	×						×			×
Mordcha			×						×	×	×					×			×	
Perchik			×				×		×		×		×							
Shandel									×							×				
Fyedka					×				×								×	×		
Sasha									×		×									
Russians					×	×					×								×	
Constable						×													×	
Gr. Tzeitel								×												
Fruma-Sarah								×												

are in each scene. It is useful for planning rehearsals and costume fittings or changes. It too will be updated as people are added to or dropped from scenes. At this point, it indicates only characters with lines (except in the case of Villagers). For example, Nahum is only in Act 1, prologue.

When you tape out the ground plan, include the proscenium arch (if there is one) and the stage's center line. In the sketch on the following page, the dash-and-dot lines are walls and doors in Act 1, and the evenly dashed lines represent a garden wall with a gate for Act 2. Act 3 is in solid lines—a porch and steps and a tree. The double lines indicate the proscenium arches and the center line. Note that the ground plan does not include furniture or other set pieces. Depending on the show, you might wish to include them. You can use different colors of tape to differentiate each act.

Rehearsal Props

Each company has different arrangements for rehearsal props, costumes, or set pieces. In general, though, the stage manager is responsible for gathering, presetting, and striking (removing) props used in rehearsal. You will rarely have prop runners or grips to help you until technical rehearsals, so enlist the cast whenever practical. (Equity actors—that is, those who belong to the actors' union—are not allowed to move scenery.)

For inanimate (as well as animate) objects, rehearsals are the most abusive time in a production. Props or costume pieces are used over and over again; a scene that happens only once during each performance may be run ten times in one rehearsal. Actors try different actions with sets

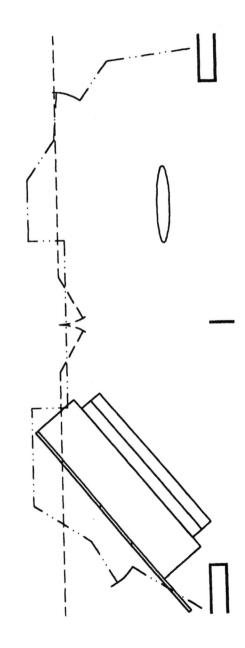

and props, finding out what works, or going over the same motions countless times. During rehearsals props may have to be packed and unpacked every night, or hauled around to different locations; during the run of the show they can usually remain in the same place. So, whenever possible, use facsimiles in rehearsal rather than the actual prop, costume, or set pieces.

Rehearsal costumes should be limited to pieces that are difficult to deal with—long skirts or capes, or pieces that are handled as props—jackets or hats that are carried around. If a prop or costume piece must be struck or set during a scene change, it is a good idea to use something to represent it; otherwise, in technical rehearsal, when props are being used and actors are moving on the set, you may find yourself trying to figure out what all that stuff is around the stage that was never cleared from the last scene.

Set pieces can be fairly vague representations as long as there is something for the actors to sit on when they need to sit. At the very least, tables and chairs should be used. Windows, doors, and stairs are left until tech rehearsal for the cast to adjust to, so it is important that the actors know what will be there, even if it is not yet in place.

Props need to be defined in rehearsal. I once worked on a disastrous production of *Candide* in which the actors mimed everything until the week of tech rehearsals. When they finally got the props (and there were many), they didn't know whether they were preset on stage or off, what to do with them when they had them, what to do with them during the musical numbers, or how to get them offstage at the end of the scene. The chaos was completely avoidable. USE PROPS IN REHEARSAL. It doesn't have to be the real thing, but the actors must have *something* to use so they can integrate it into their performance.

When the real props do appear (usually at tech rehearsals), take the time to introduce each actor to his or her props. Make sure they and the prop person know where it comes from and where it ends up, and remind them once again not to touch any prop they do not use.

One purpose of rehearsal is to repeat actions until they are set. (I've always loved the inevitable moment when the real phone is finally there and the actor ignores it completely and pantomimes it as he has during rehearsal.) So make sure the actors are rehearsing the right motions. Otherwise someone will pull the doorknob off because he's been pulling the imaginary door *in* for two weeks and it actually opens *out*.

Who's Who in the Production

The stage manager works with—or at the very least crosses the path of—everyone in a production. The lighting operator may never speak to the choreographer, the actors may not know the carpenters, but the stage manager will deal with all of them. In many cases you are the connection between production personnel: the one who communicates the wishes of the choreographer to the lighting operator, or the carpenter's concerns to the actors. Your relationship to each participant will change depending on the individuals, but here are some general guidelines as to who's who in a show and what you may expect.

DIRECTOR

Each director is different. Each one will expect different skills from a stage manager. Some want your opinions and thoughts, others don't. Some will expect you to work independently in giving notes to the cast. Other directors want you to give *them* the notes, so that they can deliver them. (Notes are comments the director jots down during rehearsals or performances that document needed changes or information that affects anyone in the show. The stage manager and various other individuals also take and give notes. Notes are covered in greater detail in Chapter 2.)

Discover the director's style. It is his or her vision you are helping to create. In most theatres, once the show opens, the stage manager runs the show and the director bows out. (In some theatres, though, they never bow out.) The transition from director to stage manager will be easier if you really understand what the director wants. It is your job to maintain the show the director built.

ACTORS AND ACTRESSES

> [*While dealing with the subject of rehearsal, a few words may be aptly said on the relations existing between the actors and the stage manager. On the professional stage the stage manager's authority is supreme. He is the umpire, against whom there is no appeal. The advantage of this is obvious. It is productive of perfect order among the actors and of an evenness and unity in the play itself. Moreover—and how important is this with amateurs—it prevents all disputes.*]

Actors and actresses depend on the stage manager. They need to be able to trust you, and will put amazing amounts of trust in you if they can. They must know you will be there, and that their props, costumes, sound cues, and light cues will be there, every single rehearsal and performance.

Performers are the only part of a production that can carry on without the other parts. You can run a show with no lights or set or costumes, or even without a script, but without actors and actresses it ceases to exist. The director may be the architect, but actors are the foundation. It's not too much for a cast to expect a working set, props in the right place, accurate time calls, and consistent cues.

They need to have a secure framework in which to produce their art. They need the stage to be the same physical setting for every performance. Understanding and accepting their need for consistency should motivate you to make sure that certain things are where the actor expects them to be.

A major style difference among performers is the consistency of the performance itself. Some actors want a great deal of flexibility to change the way they play things, depending on the audience, or how they feel, or how a fellow player performs. Others expect the exact same responses from the rest of the cast every night and won't change a line reading or expression from dress rehearsal on. You may be the referee when actors of different persuasions have to play a scene together. The director settles such differences only in rehearsal; after the show opens, the stage manager is usually in charge. Try to get the battling performers to compromise; you will never convince one side or the other that the opposing philosophy is correct.

Once a show opens, the cast needs to know about even the smallest variations before they go onstage. If something must be adjusted, a different costume or set piece used, make sure everyone involved in the affected scene knows. Doing their job well depends on their being prepared, and being made aware of changes is an important part of that preparation.

Actors also need to know limitations and guidelines. Being quiet backstage, not talking until the director is finished with notes, and keeping food and drinks off the prop table may seem obvious, but they won't happen without reminders. The rules need to be established by the stage manager before chaos reigns.

It is vital that you establish a rapport with the cast. Learn their names at the first rehearsal. (I once joined a show at tech rehearsals and had to familiarize myself with a chorus of fifty. I dutifully made mental notes: "Shirley—tall blond, pink shirt. Jennifer—jeans and sweatshirt, curly brown hair. Yvonne—braids, thin, glasses. Emily—short, blond, black t-neck and pants." Of course, at the next rehearsal they wore different clothes, and I had to start all over.) Your relationship with the cast is key. You need their trust and respect, and that's hard to develop if you keep your distance.

You will exercise all your diplomatic skills with the cast. The stage manager is expected to be mediator for differences of opinion. Actors and actresses will come to you when other performers are stepping on their lines or laughs. They will come to you to complain that so-and-so is ruining the scene because she is crossing too soon or too late or not at all. They will tell you all about how if so-and-so could just do it the way they *told* him to do it, the scene would be much better.

Listen attentively, but don't pass judgment on the criticized performer. Chances are that by the end of the show you will hear from that very person about how awful the original complainer is. Watch the scene yourself to decide what is really happening. In cases where it is justified, go to the person who is stepping on lines or moving incorrectly and ask him or her to clean up whatever is being done wrong. You'll learn when to ignore a note and when to pass it on. But when you do give the note, present it as your own idea; don't say, "so-and-so says you're holding too long for that laugh, so pick up your cue"—unless so-and-so happens to be the director. It is the stage manager's job to give notes, and you must be willing to say things to people that they don't necessarily agree with or want to hear. Just remember how you feel when *you* are corrected and, in turn, correct people gently. The nicest compliment I ever received was from an actor who told me, "You can tell someone to quit being a jerk without making him feel like a jerk." Be careful not to be personally critical or condescending when giving notes. Give notes privately unless it is something the whole cast needs to hear.

Try to nip problems in the bud. When you realize an actor (or crew person) is chronically late, tell him to be more prompt politely and in private. Ask him to show respect for the rest of the company by being on time. If that doesn't work, use mild public harassment ("Gee, thanks for joining us"). It probably won't work if reason didn't, but it will let the rest of the cast know that being late is not appropriate. It goes without saying that you must set a sterling example by being punctual yourself.

Let the cast and crew know what your expectations are from the very beginning. When I call "places," I want to see movement. I expect actors to stop anything they are doing and get on stage. I also expect acknowledgment for my calls—just any sign of recognition. And if I don't get it I will address the individual by name until he gets the message. (My fantasy is to print up elegant little cards that say, "The honor of your presence is requested on stage," and hand them out when called for.) Let the company know in rehearsals what you expect. Don't get angry with someone who fails to do something he doesn't even know he should do.

For the sake of your mental health, learn to deal effectively with prima donnas. Temperamental theatre people may be very insecure. Giving them extra attention may be the easiest way to keep things running smoothly. Consider taking time to show a difficult actor his props or how a particular part of the set that affects him works. Check with the imperious leading lady before you call places. If she isn't ready, you may wish to remind her that she is holding things up. But always be polite in letting her know that she might like to give the rest of the company the respect they deserve. If she *is* ready, she may appreciate your courtesy enough to do it more often. At the same time, don't be a doormat or tolerate abuse. Juggling the egos in a theatre company is a fine balancing act. Prima donnas may act the way they do because it gets them special treatment. Be courteous and civil (as you should with everyone involved in the show), but don't encourage poor behavior by rewarding it. Let actors know when they cause a delay in rehearsal or when they step outside the bounds of decorum by giving notes to other performers.

Your closest relationship is to the cast. Guide them through rehearsals and support them in performance.

SET DESIGNER

The set designer designs all the scenery for the show. Often the designer is also the scenic artist—the person who paints the set. Designers have a wide spectrum of styles. Some are technically oriented, others are not. Some work closely with the director, others don't. Some do meticulous drawings for the technical director in plenty of time for the set to be built. Others make sketches on cocktail napkins and change elements in the set up to the very last minute. Hopefully the set designer will create ground plans (blueprints showing how the set is laid out) and/or renderings (painted pictures of each scene) or models (three dimensional and built to scale) to give an approximation of what the set will look like when finished. Study these ground plans, renderings, or models. Learn as much as you can from the designer about how the set will work.

LIGHTING DESIGNER

The lighting designer decides where the lighting instruments will be placed, what colors they will be, when each instrument turns on and off, and what intensity it will be when it is on. The part of this you care about most is the cues—where in the dialogue or action the lights change. Find a time before technical rehearsals begin to get your light cues from the designer. Do not try to write them in as a tech rehearsal goes along. Expect changes on a nightly basis, up to and—depending on the designer—through opening night.

COSTUME DESIGNER

The costume designer is responsible for dressing the cast in a way that will delineate and enhance their characters. He or she may create designs, choose fabric, and have the costumes sewn, or may buy or rent costumes. The costume designer may be assisted by a costumer (who oversees the process), cutters, and stitchers. In smaller companies the designer may fill all these roles. As stage manager you may have little contact with the costume designer other than making sure that actors are available for fittings during the rehearsals and accommodating quick changes.

TECHNICAL DIRECTOR

The technical director supervises all aspects of the building of the set, from reading the drawings and buying materials to setting up the scenery on stage. The technical director is responsible for making the set work and can make your job heaven or hell. Work with him or her to find out exactly how the set operates, that is, how many people it will take to move each piece during scene changes, and what specific pieces are used in each scene. Discuss the schedule for load-in (putting the set into the theatre). Find out about the theatre's intercom or headset systems. Discuss what work lights may be needed backstage. As technical rehearsals progress (more about them in Chapter 2), confirm with the technical director what set elements will be finished and when. Have him or her lead the cast through a safety tour of the set at the first technical rehearsal. Find out exactly whom to contact if something goes wrong with the set during performance. (Technical directors move the show into the theatre but are not involved in running the performances. You or the crew need to deal with set problems that occur during a show, but if there are more serious repairs needed before the next performance, you need to know whom to contact.)

LIGHTING OPERATOR

The lighting operator operates the light board that runs the lights. He or she also runs the board during technical rehearsals so that the designer can see what different cues look like. A cue may be the picture created by lights, or the point when the picture changes. Once the cue is set, the lighting operator notes the individual changes for each cue. Now that most boards are computerized, it's just a matter of inputting the cues; the board duplicates them when the "Go" button is pushed to execute each cue.

RUNNING CREW: SETS, PROPS, WARDROBE

The running crew moves scenery, sets and strikes props, or helps performers with costume changes. They usually start coming to rehearsals during tech week. You may have to organize the scene changes. If so, be prepared to have crew assignments (who does what when) ready before technical rehearsals. (See Chapter 2.)

MUSIC DIRECTOR/CONDUCTOR

The music director conducts the orchestra and may work with the actors and singers in rehearsals to help them learn their music (sometimes a vocal coach is given that responsibility). The conductor impacts your job several ways. Many light and set-change cues will be called in time with the music. Your cues will be more accurate if you follow the conductor. Knowing how to read or count music is helpful for musicals and mandatory for stage managing opera. For a nonmusical, the stage manager controls the timing, but for musicals or operas, he or she runs the show with the conductor. The conductor calls the orchestra together to tune, and he or she will give the cue (downbeat) that starts each act.

CHOREOGRAPHER

The choreographer arranges the dancing in the show. You may have very little to do with the choreographer, since you don't usually have to record blocking during dance numbers. But you will want to note where the dancers are at the beginning and end of each musical number.

As a stage manager you will work with exciting, creative, funny, aggravating, spontaneous personalities, people who, however brief the contact, will become part of your life forever. Energy, creative spirit, and camaraderie make theatre the special art that it is. And working with everyone on the production staff makes stage managing the special job that it is.

❧[2]❧

Rehearsals

THE following list will vary from theatre to theatre and show to show, but generally these are the stage manager's responsibilities during rehearsals.

1. Unlock and lock up the rehearsal area or theatre. You are the first to arrive and the last to leave. This gives you built-in time to do little projects or repair work, or pre-set for the next show while you wait for the rehearsal to start or performers to get out of costume after a show.

2. Set up the rehearsal area. If the first rehearsal is a read-through, have a table with the correct number of chairs already around it. (At a read-through rehearsal, actors read their lines with no accompanying movements.) Once the actors are on their feet, set up an approximation of the scene being worked on with tables, chairs, benches, or whatever is available, and have rehearsal props accessible. While actors are still carrying their scripts ("on book"), they may not want to deal with props, but as soon as they are off book make sure they have something to work with.

3. In your "prompt script," take precise notes *in pencil* of all the moves the director tells the performers to make.

These moves are called blocking. Changes will be made as the rehearsals progress, so always take blocking notes in pencil and make sure you have spare pencils as well as a good eraser.

4. Stay "on book," which means follow the script, so that you are ready to read a line to any actor who "goes up" (forgets). You may also be called upon to read the lines of an actor who is not at rehearsal.

5. Keep track of the next scene to be rehearsed, so you can set up for it quickly and make sure the actors needed are in the vicinity.

6. Fake practical sound cues (doorbells, phones, gunshots). Call light cues such as blackouts and lights up to define the scene and help set it in your own mind.

7. Take notes on potential problems or changes in the set or props. Communicate these changes or problems to the appropriate production personnel.

8. Time scenes once they are running without stops, and jot down the times for future reference.

Building the Prompt Book

> [*He had then better prepare a special inter-leaved prompt book of the play, marking in diagrams the positions and movements of the characters and their attitudes in the various tableaux; all this should be done before the first rehearsal. This copy must contain also a "property plot," i.e., a list of properties to be used, their position, and nature of the furniture, etc. Property noises, i.e., ring of bells, thunder, sound of broken glass, laughter, etc.,*

had better be underlined in red ink, also the different points at which characters are to be called, so as to render the prompter's task easier.]

Throughout the rehearsal process you are building your prompt book. The prompt book is the brain of the show. It is sacred. It consists of the script with blocking written clearly in pencil, contact lists for cast and production staff, rehearsal schedule and worksheets (during rehearsal), and, by opening night, final versions of the scene change, prop, light, and costume plots. Any stage manager should be able to run a totally unfamiliar show with the prompt book alone. A new actor should be able to go into any role by its direction. During rehearsals it must be correct and up to date at all times. It is your job to know everything, and your best tool is the prompt book.

Keeping track of the blocking is one of your most important tasks. It is vital that you get every move down accurately. If you miss something, go back over it with the director. Your script should be the production's blueprint and should have in it every move that every actor makes. You should use a fairly standard code: for characters, use the first initial of the character's name with a circle around it so that it's easy to pick out on the page. X means cross (which is basically any movement), US or U for upstage (away from the audience), DS or D for downstage (toward the audience), SL or L for stage left (the actor's left; this is tricky if you sit facing the actors in rehearsal), SR or R for stage right (the actor's right), and C for center stage. v means sit and ∧ means stand. You can use combinations of the above. For example: USC (upstage center), DSR (downstage right), DC (down center), UR (up right). It helps to indicate a piece of furniture for clarification, as in Ⓦ X R to ch ∨ (for Walter cross right to chair and sit) or Ⓛ∧X UL to tbl (for Lulu stand and cross upleft to table). Use arrows to indicate intricate patterns or to show if someone crosses below (downstage of) a set piece ∟ or above (upstage of) a set piece ⌐, and the direction of the movement. The prompt script must be accurate and should be able to resolve any arguments about blocking. (See Appendix VII for examples.)

Staying on book after the actors have put their scripts down demands a great deal of concentration on your part. You must literally follow every line of the script. (Trust me, the second you take your eyes off the page someone will call for a line and you won't know where you are.) Of course, you also have to keep an eye on the blocking while watching the script. And occasionally answer someone's questions (use your own judgment on this—you may decide not to let anyone talk to you when you are on book). When you do give a line you must be loud enough to be heard without disrupting the flow of the scene. Read just enough to jog the actor's memory; don't try to give the whole line or speech. You should also wait until he or she says "line." If you jump in before he requests it, he may get angry because he was just acting and knew his next line. You may have to remind the cast that when they go off book (stop carrying their scripts) they should call for a line by simply saying "line." Otherwise, when they go up they will either apologize and break everyone's concentration, or just say nothing and expect you to come in with the line, which will also break everyone's concentration. If you are lucky, you will develop the ESP it takes to stay on book effectively.

Props or set pieces will be added or struck as rehearsals progress, so the plots you created to use in rehearsal and the actual running plots will probably be very different animals. (Compare the first rehearsal worksheet from Chapter 1 with the final scene change plot in Appendix V and the final prop plot in Appendix VI.) Sometimes designers will do the final running plots for sets, props, and costumes, but if they don't, then you must. By opening night the plots must be accurate and up to date. It's your problem if the prop person gets sick and you find yourself at a performance wondering where the rubber pork chop and the electric toothbrush go. The plots should be clear enough for someone who was not at rehearsal to run the show from them.

Throughout rehearsals you will continue filling in the details, which will change with amazing frequency. Make notes of everything in your script—which side of the stage hand props come from, what gets preset, whether or not light fixtures are functional (if so, are the lights on or off at the top of the scene?), whether doors or windows are open or closed, and so on. Each show is different, so it's difficult to list all the variables here, but you'll learn what to look for. As soon as possible, get light and sound cues from the lighting designer and/or director. Run practical sound cues in rehearsal by verbalizing the bang of a gunshot or the crash of breaking dishes.

Information Hub

You will also need to act as a conduit for information for the production staff. The most efficient way to do this is at production meetings. If you work in a company that doesn't have production meetings, talk to the director or designers about having them. Be ready to run them yourself, if necessary. The director, tech director, stage manager, all designers, the music director, and the choreographer should attend. Each production staff member is asked how things are going, what progress has been made, what still needs to be done. Discuss costume fittings: are actors called before, after, or during rehearsals? Find out who is on the running crew or how many people it will take to operate the set. Raise sticky questions (in front of witnesses), such as, "I noticed the leading lady leaps onto the coffee table during her big number—isn't that an original Louis XIV piece we're borrowing from the museum?" Find out when publicity photo calls are scheduled, who's in them, what is needed in the way of props or costumes, and where they're taking place, if not on the set.

If you don't have production meetings, you still need to pass on information regarding many details of the production, so be prepared for a good many individual consultations. Are quick-change booths needed? If so, who is building them and where will they be located? Who assigns the cast to dressing rooms? What are you using for prop tables? Where will they go? Some of this is pretty standard if you work in the same space for every show. Even so, the set can create limitations, and tech rehearsal is too late to find out that no one can get to their props.

Ask the director anything you need to know. Until

you've worked with someone long enough to second-guess him, assume you know nothing. To have a cohesive production you must understand the director's underlying philosophy as well as more mundane concepts such as what is needed for rehearsal space. It is the director's vision that is being created, so if you don't want to spend a lot of time doing things over, you will find out what the director wants and carry it out. You also have the director's authority to back you up. The quickest way to quell arguments is to say, "Talk to the director, I'm just doing what she wants."

Learn about the set from the designer. "How does the drop work? Where is its line? Which way do the doors open? How does that wagon lock? How many people does it take to move that platform?" No one will volunteer this information. Most of it will be in the drawings, so take the time to study them. Visit the shop while the set is being built so you can see things in various states. If something looks like it won't stand up to the director's expectations— it's too small or too large or too heavy—talk to the designer about it or ask the director to do so. Unless the designer is at rehearsals (highly unlikely), he may not know about that great new piece of action that depends on the heroine swinging from the chandelier, or the villain bursting through the roof.

Sharing information in the early stages helps avoid later panic. The operational word here is *share*. You're all in this together, so listening and staying nonjudgmental can help make this part of the process an open forum for dealing with problems and developing solutions. When in doubt, *ask*. You can't ask too many questions. You need to know every aspect of a show, and that knowledge won't come to you by osmosis.

A frequent problem for stage managers is getting stuck in the middle of differing opinions. The director wants one thing, the designer another, and both expect you to carry out their wishes. The director is ultimately in charge of the show and always wins. But be as diplomatic as possible when explaining that to the designer (the show isn't open yet, and you don't need all-out war). If possible, bring up the problem when the director and designer are together, or get them together so you can. If not, tell the designer you're going along with the director's wishes until you hear otherwise.

You are expected to be an encyclopedia for the cast. But never be afraid to say, "I don't know." Don't put yourself on the line if you don't know—people will never trust you if they get too many wrong answers. But along with saying you don't know is the obligation to go find the answer, or tell them whom to talk with if that's more appropriate.

Do your homework. Study the script. Review the ground plans or model and be prepared to explain the set to the actors. With a very complicated set, the earlier you tell the cast what to expect, the better off you will be when you move on stage. If they have only three or four rehearsals on the set, you can help them adjust to the set more quickly by talking them through it ahead of time. For instance, tell them where to exit at the end of a scene so they won't be running into the wagon that's moving on or the wall that's flying in.

Accept responsibility for knowing as much as you can and sharing it with everyone who needs to know. Impart information in the most efficient, direct way possible, and pay attention to the response to see if further action is needed on your part. Stage managing is a hub through which information flows and is rerouted to the places that need it. The stage manager has fingers in all the pies and should know all the elements that go into the unique organism that every production becomes. The director may not have the faintest idea how the technical end works, and the lighting designer may not give a hoot about an actor's motivation, but the stage manager must understand every part of the show and how it relates to the other parts in order to run the show properly.

Timing

The timing of all meetings, rehearsals, and performances is the stage manager's responsibility. You are the company clock. Starting all production-related events on time falls under your jurisdiction as well as keeping track of time while they are happening. It's your job to say, "Let's get going, please." If you hang out sipping coffee and chatting with the actors before rehearsal, it may never start because no one else takes the initiative.

Be concise and verbal about time. Announce the end of breaks clearly. Know how much needs to be covered in a rehearsal period and help the director see that it gets done. Don't let scene shifts take longer than necessary. Have things ready to move on stage for the next scene. If actors or others are discussing matters that could just as well be talked about after rehearsal or during a production meeting, suggest to the parties involved that they do so.

But in this, as in all things, your approach should be flexible. During rehearsals, learn when to let something be worked on "until we get it right" and when to move the action forward. You may need to prod the director by asking,

"Can we go on?" As soon as she is ready, give the company a starting point in the script at which to do so. But don't be fanatic about running without stops. After all, the point of this is *rehearsal,* which is doing things until they are right. So don't expect everything to fall in line with your game plan.

Tech Rehearsals

The rehearsals during which the actors move onto the set and use the actual props are called technical or tech rehearsals. There are several types, and theatres use different combinations of them.

Paper Tech: The stage manager gets lighting cues from the lighting designer and scene change cues from the technical director or set designer. The director attends, but the actors do not.

Dry Tech: It takes place on the set with no actors. All the light cues are run in sequence to view them on the appropriate sets.

Cue to Cue: The show is run one light cue or set change at a time to see how the cue or set change works, using actors but cutting (not performing) songs or dialogue between the cues.

Full Tech: The entire show is run with all parts except costumes and orchestra.

Dress Rehearsal: All elements are used without an audience. Every effort is made to run the show without stops.

Technical rehearsals are generally long and frustrating. Plan to double the running time of the show in order to tech it. It is vitally important for the stage manager and the production staff to set specific goals for technical rehearsals. Are you setting light cues? That can mean adjusting the levels of the instruments as well as setting the timing of the cue itself. The adjustments must then be recorded. (If you had a dry tech, this wouldn't be as time consuming, but changes are always needed once the actors are in the scene.) Is the goal to establish smooth scene changes? Or is it a run for continuity—to see all the pieces together without stopping? Once goals are set, an evaluation after the rehearsal is also necessary. Review what was actually accomplished and what problems need to be worked out at the next rehearsal. Tech rehearsals can be difficult and seemingly aimless. It is important for all those involved to know that headway is being made.

Starting tech rehearsals on time is a challenge because the carpenters or lighting people may be working on the set. But it can be done, regardless of the scoffing of theatre people everywhere, if you are willing to take charge and do a little pushing. (Remember to push with a gentle and polite but firm attitude.) Begin in production meetings by letting people know you plan to stick to the schedule. Discuss problems such as meal breaks and time-consumers such as sound checks. Once a tech rehearsal schedule has been established (by you, if not by the director or designer), confirm it with everyone concerned so there's no chance of "But I thought . . ." Create a schedule for yourself for clearing the stage, sweeping, and presetting the set and props. If the director must run things on stage before rehearsal starts, make time for that. Don't wait and be surprised. At the end of the rehearsal, ask what is planned for the next.

If you estimate presetting will take an hour, go to the technical director two hours before starting time and say, "Please clear the set in one hour." Whether you will be able to set pieces and start on time is always uncertain. Important set or electrical functions won't be ready in spite of the director's begging or the tech director's assurances that they will be. At some point the director must make the decision whether to go on without them or not. It should be the stage manager's decision, but in nonprofessional theatre the director is usually still in charge at this point. So ask her. Make sure the decision is made, and tell everyone what will or won't be there. If it's important enough to wait for, then do so, but take the late start into consideration immediately, and find out what the director wants to cut to make up for the lost time. Don't let the delay dissolve into recriminations and even more wasted time.

Don't expect anyone but you to watch the clock. Tell the crew when to clear the working equipment, and give them time to set the stage. Tell the prop crew when to set their props. And while you're at it, remind the director, so she can have her notes ready on time. Give the cast and orchestra appropriate calls. In general, my line to everyone at tech rehearsals is, "The sooner we start, the sooner we finish."

Keeping things moving during tech and dress rehearsals is vital. If the cast, crew, and musicians are accustomed to prompt calls and start times, they will follow that pattern. If they think, "I don't have to hurry, we never start on time anyway," it will be much harder to do so.

Set Changes

[*One source of great annoyance to the audience in amateur performances is the long waits which invariably occur during changes of scene. The stage manager must spare no pains to make the events of the evening follow quickly on each other. If there is a musical part between pieces he must use every endeavor to urge the conductor to be prompt in his action, and to get the chorus quickly on and off the stage. Musical people are generally leisurely in their movements, and unless urged on will occupy so long a time over their various items as to frustrate all endeavours to be up to time. Whatever plan is adopted, there should be a scenic or property rehearsal to avoid any possible misunderstanding or mistake. In this rehearsal, those members of the company at liberty at this part of the play should each be entrusted with a definite number of properties, both of those to be carried off the stage, and those to be moved on. They should know exactly where the latter are stowed, so as to be able to find them at once, and exactly the position on the stage in which they are to be placed.]*

The management of set changes is done by different people in almost every theatre: the director, technical director, scene shift crew chief, or stage manager. If no one else does it, the responsibility goes to the stage manager by default. It's for your own peace of mind that you make sure that individual crew people are assigned to scenery shifts before the first rehearsal with set changes. If someone else makes the assignments, review their work to make sure everything is covered. Nothing is more aggravating, or more avoidable, than having to stop the action to decide who moves what during a tech rehearsal. Expect adjustments once you are actually running the scene changes.

Before technical rehearsals begin, call a meeting with the tech director or scene designer to review every set piece that is moved in the course of the show. (This might be done during a paper tech.) For each shift, find out what set pieces fly (that is, are raised or lowered by rope lines), roll, or are carried, and how many people it takes to do each task. If someone else is managing the scene changes, ideally he would come to this meeting. Whether he does or not, as stage manager you still need this information.

If you are in charge of assigning shifts, after this meeting review your list of set changes and your list of crew people, and decide who does what. This becomes the shift plot. (For a shift plot of *42nd Street*, see Appendix V.)

Make enough copies of the scene-change plot so that you can give one to every member of the crew. On each person's copy, highlight that person's name each time it appears. Also be certain that you mark in your prompt script the warnings, standbys, and "Go" cues for each shift.

Shifts are cued in different ways. Sometimes the crew chief is on headset. Sometimes the cue is visual: raising your arm is "standby" and lowering it is "go." There may be a cueing system with small lights on the theatre wall above the pinrail: light on is "standby," light off is "go." You may use a combination of ways.

Call the crew early for the first rehearsal with set changes so that you can hand out their assignment sheets and discuss each change. Show them the set and how each piece is supposed to work. Tell them how they will be cued.

This meeting of fifteen to thirty minutes can save hours of wasted time during the rehearsal.

The first time through, plan to stop the action after a change has been made in order to find out if it worked. Take notes on needed corrections (and later make sure they are recorded on the appropriate crew member's copies of the plot), and rerun the shift if necessary. If the show is very complicated, without much rehearsal time on stage, consider having a separate scene-change rehearsal with just the crew.

If you are working with a technical director or crew chief who will do all this for you, don't forget to thank them after every single tech rehearsal and performance.

When the final positions of each piece have been determined during the rehearsal, and before the next shift takes place, mark each piece's location by placing a dot of colored tape on the stage floor. This is called spiking the set pieces. Color code the spike marks by act. Spike on the upstage side of the piece, and be sure to mark both the US/DS position and the SL/SR position. For example, spike where both the upstage chair legs go. If you spike only one, you won't know if the chair goes on the onstage (toward center) mark or the offstage (away from center) mark.

If the shifts are done in total blackouts, you may need to use fluorescent (glow) tape for spike marks. The glow is activated by light. Be conservative when using it onstage or you may get a runway effect when the lights go out. Assign crew members to spike before the rehearsal, one stage right and one stage left, so they can be ready with tape and interrupt the rehearsal as little as possible. Glow tape is very useful offstage to mark escape steps, railings, and edges of platforms. Don't be conservative here. Someone may need to be assigned to shine a flashlight on the tape before blackouts if your backstage area is very dim.

Actors should not be responsible for moving scenery because they have enough to keep track of during a performance. But sometimes the actor's help is an integral part of the show (*Candide* comes to mind, and *The Elephant Man*), and sometimes it is necessary in community theatre when there aren't enough volunteers. If actors are doing the scene changes, assign their set responsibilities along with the blocking so that actors can write them in their scripts and run them (even in pantomime) in rehearsals. Be ready to choreograph them if the director doesn't. Don't wait until the last minute. It's not fair to expect actors to learn them during tech week—they are too busy adjusting to the set and costumes. If you work the set changes out ahead of time and get the director's cooperation in presenting and rehearsing them, you might not have a disastrous opening night.

For really complicated shifts, do little quizzes. Have everyone involved talk through exactly what they do, then ask questions: Who moves the table? Who strikes the chair? Who sets which props? In what order? Have everyone visualize it and make sure people *really* know what to do. It takes time, but in the long run it's quicker than people bumping into each other.

Make sure the dressers have rehearsed or at least talked through costume changes with any cast members involved in quick changes. Don't let them wait until dress rehearsal, then hold the whole show up while they try to undress and dress somebody in the dark in thirty seconds.

Notes

Notes document changes needed in the production. The director takes notes for performers to correct blocking, to suggest a different line reading, or to ask for a new acting direction. Directors use notes to fine tune an actor's performance without interrupting the rehearsal. During technical rehearsals the director takes notes on set, costume, or lighting problems. The stage manager will receive or take notes on the timing of cues or set changes. Other production personnel take notes as well. But recognize that there is a fine line between an appropriate note and an inappropriate personal opinion. The expression of too many personal opinions can lead to a judgmental, confusing, and generally unpleasant environment. This line will be crossed less often if there are firm policies about who gives notes to whom. People need to restrain themselves from giving notes when it's not appropriate to do so. Theatre is not a democracy; there is a specific pecking order. During rehearsals the director is omnipotent. After the director come the various designers, choreographers, and conductors or musical directors who are generally on the same level (depending on personal power and/or politics), then the stage manager and technical director, followed by crew heads and chorus leads, with carpenters, stitchers, actors, and others bringing up the rear. If you have a producer, the director and conductor both answer to the producer and may be on a more equal footing with each other; but without a producer, the conductor usually answers to the director.

When the show opens, the balance shifts away from the director and designers to the stage manager (and, if you are doing a musical, with the conductor as guardian angel, if

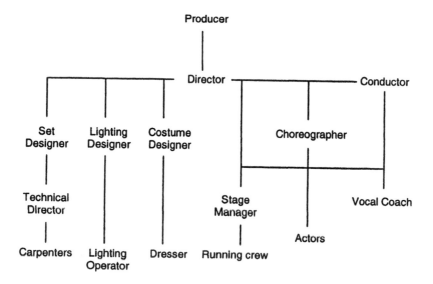

you're lucky—the conductor can direct the orchestra to vamp [that is, keep repeating a musical phrase] during shift problems on stage). During rehearsals, notes are given according to area and place in the hierarchy. For example, the choreographer gives notes to the dancers, but if he has a problem with the singers, he discusses it with the music director, not with the singers directly. Once the show opens, all notes should go through the stage manager. Actors or crew members should never give each other notes. When they have a problem, they should talk to the stage manager, who then gives the note to the appropriate person.

Speeches

> [*He should then post up any rules he particularly wishes observed during the performance.*

> *The following will generally be found impor-*
> *tant—*
>
> *Gentlemen are Requested—*
> I. *Not to stand at the wings or passages, es-*
>   *pecially at the prompt entrance, during*
>   *the course of the play unless waiting for*
>   *their cues.*
> II. *Under no circumstances whatever to*
>   *speak to the prompter whilst the curtain*
>   *is up.*
> III. *To answer the summons of the call-boy*
>   *immediately.*
> IV. *To watch silently and attentively for their*
>   *cues of entrances.*
> V. *Not to go upon the stage, or move any*
>   *properties between the acts, except at the*
>   *request of the stage manager or scene*
>   *shifters.*
> *Then there may be some particular rules in*
> *reference to the plays themselves.*]

From the very beginning, the stage manager must let people know what is expected of them, even if it seems redundant. (Repetition is an effective way to teach.) Actors and technicians may need to be reminded, "When you're backstage, if you can see the audience, they can see you," regardless of how obvious it sounds.

The following speeches can be used for specific occasions, such as the first day of rehearsal, the first time with props, first tech, and so on. Tailor them for different companies or theatres, but the message will stay pretty much the same. Don't take for granted that because you know something, everyone else does too. These speeches may sound pretty silly to you the twentieth time you deliver them, but they help get the job done, which is running a smoother, more polished production.

FIRST REHEARSAL

This is your first opportunity to let the cast get to know you. Be friendly. Speak clearly. Look people in the eye. Set the tone—authoritative but not aggressive. Outline theatre policies regarding complimentary tickets, visitors at rehearsal, makeup (whether or not they need to provide it), costume fitting arrangements, and photo calls. Some of these topics may be covered by other people; if so, don't repeat the information, but make sure these areas are covered by someone. Tell the cast the time and location of all rehearsals, the date when they must be off book, when tech rehearsals start, and especially all performance dates and calls. (The *call* is the time the performers, crew, and musicians must be at the theatre.)

FIRST TIME WITH PROPS

"Don't touch any props but the ones you actually use. Return props to the prop table, or let the prop person know if you can't so that he or she can. Don't put anything except props on the prop table, especially not drinks. Don't eat prop food unless you are directed to do so, and then only as part of rehearsal. If you have a problem, tell the stage manager. Don't tell the prop runner about great ideas you have for new props, or things you think you need that aren't in the script." This speech can sound very negative with all those "don'ts," so be sure it is delivered in a friendly, "of course, I know none of you would ever do these things" manner, rather than bawling out the cast before they've even had a chance.

FIRST TIME WITH COSTUMES

"Hang up your costumes. Don't eat or drink in costume." Eating or drinking in costume is a very "at your own risk" area—actors may break this rule, and if they mess up they are at your mercy, but the show must go on and the costume be cleaned. If they are moving into dressing rooms before a previous cast has moved out, remind them to show the same respect for that cast's personal space as they want shown when the next cast moves in. Bring up costume cleaning procedures and tell them to keep the dressing room clean enough that it won't be condemned by the health department. If the show is a musical, you might even bring up the need to use deodorant. This is obviously a sensitive area, but sometimes it is necessary, and it's a lot easier to tell the whole cast than to discuss it in private with the offender(s).

FIRST TECH REHEARSAL

The important points of this speech are outlining the schedule (cue to cue or run through); asking them to stay close to be ready to rerun scenes (especially beginnings and endings); and introducing them to the set by going over safety problems, explaining how things work, and telling them what is and isn't finished. Sincerely ask for everyone's patience and remind everyone that while the actors have been rehearsing for weeks, the running crews have only two or three tries to learn their parts, and it's their turn now. I also emphasize this to my crew. They have to pick up their jobs very quickly, so patience and concentration are vital.

On opening night, try to keep speeches to a bare minimum—if possible, just "Have fun out there and have a good show."

Closing night calls for the obligatory speech about not playing jokes during performance. They are never as funny to the audience as to those on stage, and this audience has paid just as much as every other and wants to see the same show that everyone else saw.

Different shows or theatres will call for different speeches. Always remember that just because you've been with a company forever and know the routine, the actors may not. Some will, some won't. Everyone will benefit from hearing the ground rules on a regular basis.

·{ 3 }·

Performance

YOU'VE survived rehearsals, and the show is ready to open. Now the fun begins! Running performances should become routine, which may feel good after the constant changes of rehearsal. But don't let the routine lull you into complacency. Follow these guidelines for every performance.

1. Make sure the crew is at the theatre.

2. Check the set and prop presets and do an instrument check with the lighting operator.

3. Confirm that the headsets and running lights are working.

4. Sweep or mop the stage.

5. Check the sign-in sheet to see that the actors are there. The sign-in sheet is a chart that you make with each cast person's name on it and blank spaces for every performance. It is very similar to the character detail worksheet, only put the performance dates across the top instead of the scene numbers (Appendix IV). If you have a large running crew, they should be on it too.

6. Give the actors their time calls—at half-hour (thirty

minutes before curtain), fifteen minutes, five minutes, and places (one or two minutes before curtain).

7. Collect the cast's valuables and put them in a locked, safe place.

8. See that the set is ready in time for the house to open. Before it opens, notify the actors so that they will stay off the set if there is no curtain. Let the house manager know when you are ready. Be especially sure to let the house manager know if there are any problems which might delay the opening of the house.

9. Call places for the orchestra when you call five minutes for the cast.

10. Turn work lights off and running lights on.

11. Call all light, sound, and set-change cues, including deck and fly cues.

12. Stay on book through the whole performance. You may think you have it memorized two weeks into the show, but never get complacent. *Always follow book no matter how easy the show or how long the run.* It is your guiding light.

13. Solve, on the spot, the innumerable crises which befall every production.

14. Have fun.

Calling the Show

[*The prompter's work is both tedious and tiring. A good prompter is a rara avis. . . . He should allow nothing to draw his attention from the play. The commonest pitfall of all prompters is watching the stage instead*

*of the book. He should never take his eyes
from the latter without marking the place
with his finger. He should kill all feeling, and
remain perfectly impassive, though the actors
be convulsed with laughter or the audience in
tears.*

*If there is a break in the lines . . . a sharp
prompter will tell at once from the expression
on the actor's face, if his services are required,
or the pause is intentional. It is astonishing
how few prompters pursue any rational plan,
and can be depended on in the hour of need.*]

There are countless ways to call a show; some are more effective than others. Here are some suggestions.

Pay attention. Write warnings and standbys as well as cues in your prompt book, and stay with the book even if it is your ninety-seventh performance of a ten-cue show. Shows with few cues may in fact be harder to do well. It's difficult to stay on your toes while you are waiting fifteen or twenty minutes for the next cue, but you must do it. Pay attention to the stage as well as your script. Nothing is more embarrassing than waking up from a reverie when someone asks, "Isn't there a cue here?" or "What's all that purple light?" If the operator is running a manual light board when a light cue goes wrong, he may not even know it because he is concentrating on his hands, the cue sheets, and the dimmers. If so, tell him calmly, "You might want to bring something up stage right—the actors are talking in the dark." Keep an eye on the stage even when your eyes are glued to the script because you have to call eight sound cues and eleven light cues in the next thirty seconds. You will get used to this split vision in rehearsal while simultaneously staying on book and watching blocking.

Be consistent. Call cues in the same place and in the same way every time. It may be boring, but it's only fair. The operator and crew must be able to rely on you if they are to do their jobs well.

Be concise. An easy pattern is "Warning cue 1," spoken about a page of dialogue before the cue; "Standby cue 1," about four lines before the cue; and "Cue 1 go," with "go" being the signal for the operator to start the cue. (With computerized boards, warnings aren't always necessary. If the operator is simply pushing a "Go" button to activate the cue, he needs only a standby.) If a show has light and sound, always distinguish between the two—such as "Light cue 1" and "Sound cue 3." Using letters for one and numbers for the other may also help ("Light cue 1" and "Sound cue A"), but if you are also calling fly cues and scenery shifts, you may as well use numbers for everything. Use the warning to go over sequences if they are complicated, or to remind the operator of a "visual cue." If a cue is taken off the action on stage (rather than a line or musical note), and the stage manager can't see it but the operator can, then call it as a visual cue. You would say, "Warning" (or "Standby") "cue 13. It's visual when Wagner gets off the wagon." Warn five or six cues at once if they are close together. If necessary, rehearse sequences against a stopwatch to make sure you can handle the linguistic gymnastics necessary to get the words out fast enough and in the right order.

Headsets are intimate pieces of equipment. Each person wearing one is at the mercy of everyone else on the system. Don't ever make loud noises into the microphone. This includes chewing (especially noisy food), heavy breathing, coughing, sneezing, or shouting to the cast on stage. Turn your microphone off before you take off your headset; if you leave it on, when you lay down the headset it will make loud and obnoxious noises and continue to pick up any activity around you. Address people by name, particularly when there are more than three people on headset and their voices may not be easily distinguishable. Let people do their jobs—avoid extraneous chatter during tech week when the designer is trying to talk the operator through cue changes. Don't talk once standby has been called. You shouldn't talk after a warning, but like eating or drinking in costume, that's a rule that is made to be broken. Ask the operators to acknowledge cues—you don't have ESP and otherwise you won't know they are ready or even hearing you.

Well before tech week, check out the lighting system in the theatre in which you are working. Is it computerized, or is it manual with preset boards and a master? If it's computerized, what happens if the board goes out? Is there a manual override? If it is not computerized, will only one person run it or is a preset operator also needed? (Lights were a lot more fun to run in the old days, even if they couldn't be designed as intricately. Pressing a "Go" button can't compare to changing multiple dimmers in a short blackout and cross fading into a new scene.) Could you run the lights yourself in an emergency? It's a good idea to discuss how you call the show with operators and crew the first time you work with them. Let them know you want acknowledgments and how long you give for warnings. Find out what they expect or need. This is one of the closest working relationships you'll have. These are the people who

move the switches and pull the ropes when you say *go*. You
need to trust and respect each other.

You may call the show from backstage or from the light
booth. Each location has advantages and disadvantages—it
depends on the show and the theatre. If you are backstage,
you are more aware of potential problems with set changes
or actors who are not in place for entrances. And from
backstage you may be able to head off disasters. But you
may be more distracted by people interrupting while you
work, and you may not be able to see the whole set. Calling
a show from the light booth gives you a better perspective
of the whole show. A full view is necessary if you give notes
on the acting during the run. It's also important if you are
calling visual cues (cues called off action rather than dialogue). Being in the booth also isolates you so that you can
concentrate. If you call a show from the booth, have a reli-
able assistant backstage on headset to intervene in case of
crisis.

Timing

Timing the show is also the stage manager's responsibility.
After pencils and extra erasers, a stopwatch is probably the
most important stage-managing tool. Keep track of how
long scenes and acts run. You'll also need to time costume
and scene changes and reconcile how long they take with
the time available to do them. Tell the actors how long the
intermissions are. Let the house staff know how long the
acts are so they can be ready for the intermissions.

Your own internal clock will have to be finely tuned.
How long is a scene change taking? Is it running fast or

slow? If there's a problem, how much time do you have to fix it? *Always* be aware of time and keep others conscious of it as well.

Once the show opens it becomes even more important to be punctual about curtain time. Audiences can be trained. There will always be latecomers, but if subscribers and return customers know that the shows start on time, they are more likely to try to be there on time. (Some theatres have stiff policies about not seating latecomers, and I applaud them.) Coordinate timing with the house manager. The house staff may be biased toward holding (delaying) the show to accommodate late arrivals in the audience, but it is truly a producer's decision, so find out what the policy is and stick to it. You may get into trouble for starting a show on the dot of eight o'clock if the producer is still in the lounge wooing a potential donor. On the other hand, if the orchestra or union crew will go into overtime and cost the producer extra, he may want a precise curtain time and tight intermissions.

The curtain call is another example of timing within the show. If you are cuing the actors for their curtain-call entrances, keep them tight—send each actor out before the applause peaks for the previous performer. Don't give the audience a chance to slow down. When lowering and then raising the curtain for multiple calls, never let the curtain settle into place. It must barely touch the stage before bouncing back up. Nothing is worse than raising the curtain for a second or third call to dying applause (or what I call a "walking ovation," when the audience is starting to leave the theatre).

From knowing the number of seconds it takes the curtain to rise and fall, to sensing the pacing of a show and whether it is moving fast or slow, timing is one of your most important functions as a stage manager. You cannot control time, but you must always be aware of it and use that awareness to make the production work as well as you can.

Details

[*In professional theatres the call boy goes round to all the dressing rooms, at stated intervals, to call or "shout" the time at the actor's disposal. Over this performance he generally makes as much noise as possible, and his "Half an hour, gentlemen, please" or "Beginners, please" penetrates into the dressing rooms however thick the doors thereof. With amateurs this is perhaps unnecessary. [I beg to differ on this point.—LA.] Every one is on the qui vive before the rise of the curtain. The cases in which the employment of a call boy is absolutely necessary are either when a character has not to appear until some half an hour after the curtain rises, or when a character has to make a quick change. The stage manager marks in the prompt-book the point at which an actor is to be called, the prompter gives the word to the call boy, who immediately dispatches his errand. Woe to the thoughtless person who waylays him en route and produces a stage wait!*]

Be a "hands on" stage manager. See for yourself that everything is ready and that all the bodies are where they should be. If you are lucky enough to have an assistant, you may put him or her in charge of checking the sign-in sheet, but check the status at half-hour. Anyone not in the theatre by then needs a call. And make sure once the call is made, you are told the minute that performer walks in. (I started a production of *Mame* once without realizing that one of the characters in the first act wasn't at the theatre yet. He made it on time, just barely, and after I quit shaking I knew that was a mistake I'd never make again.)

Make the time calls in person. Even in a large theatre with an intercom, the cast should see your face (and you, theirs) at half-hour, fifteen, and places. If there is a problem, you won't see it if you're hiding behind a microphone. Give people a chance to talk to you. It doesn't even hurt to ask, "How's everything going?" By being available to listen to people's problems, you can get the jump on a situation before it reaches catastrophic proportions, or diffuse it entirely by letting the person blow off steam. (Of course, while you are being Miss Congeniality, make sure you don't forget the schedule.) Always know what time it is and be aware of your next call. Interrupt any conversation you are having when it's time to give one. There is no excuse for a late call.

Check the set before every performance, in person, with a detailed list of the preset. Don't just ask, "Is it ready?" but look for yourself. Nobody's perfect; anything may be forgotten, and the five or ten minutes it takes to double-check are well spent. Always use a checklist, for even the simplest show. If you are also responsible for actually doing the preset, when you think it's finished, go back over everything again with your list to see what you may have left out. Be even more vigilant about checking on matinee days. At the second show you may feel as though you have already done everything, and you will be more likely to forget something.

Many actors check their own props. Encourage this. It shows a willingness on their part to take responsibility. But ask them not to do so until after the prop person is done setting, and you have checked the props. No one should distract a prop person while they are presetting. "Why isn't my suitcase here?" is an inappropriate question if the person setting it hasn't had the chance to complete his job. Diverting the attention of the prop person during a preset is a dandy way to ensure errors.

Before the house opens (well before, in case you discover problems), go out into the audience and look at the set—from the back row as well as the front. For example, check to see that teasers and tormentors are in their correct position. You may notice things from the audience that are easy to miss on stage. If you are calling the show from the booth, you will probably see a different view of the stage than the audience sees.

No matter how careful you are, mistakes will be made. You will make them along with everyone else. I've personally pulled some real doozies—from bringing up the house lights in the middle of *Mass Appeal* to inadvertently pinning the act curtain together so it wouldn't open at the top of *Sound of Music* (talk about a Freudian slip . . .). Once I forgot the tiny demitasse spoons for the breakfast scene in *Private Lives*. Since half the laughs depended on how the actors were stirring their coffee in reaction to the dialogue, it rather changed the scene. I had to justify my existence to six performers the minute they came off stage.

Two courses of action may help when you make a mistake. First, as soon as possible, apologize to the persons affected. If you throw yourself at their feet and beg for mercy, they will respond more compassionately—usually by saying, "That's okay, we're all human." But if you wait for them to come to you—and they will—they'll be really angry and more likely to begin, "How could you be so stupid?" After all, they are in front of the audience and you are safely backstage.

Equally important to the sincere apology: as soon as you make a mistake, get over it and go on with the show. To dwell on it is to guarantee a rash of errors. Get back on track as soon as possible.

When others err, be compassionate. You too will do some horrible, stupid thing sometime and will want compassion from others. You'll also want to go bury yourself in a deep hole, and that is why you will make sure it never happens again.

Concentrating on the details pays off in a way that is hard to define. The most brilliant production will be diminished if it's sloppy. Holding for that extra second in a blackout for the ghost of the lights to disappear, or taking the extra moment to make sure all the grips are off the set after a quick change, enhances the effect of the show. The details help create the overall picture. The audience will sense it if you always strive for perfection. They may not know why the show seemed so special, but they will know it was.

Once, during a performance, an actress seated downstage leafing through a magazine, heard a lady in the front row exclaim to her husband, "Look, dear, that's the carpet I ordered" in response to a particular ad. After that, I always played to the "lady in the front row." Audiences do notice the tiniest things. They will look to see if the writing in a letter is real, if the words are actually what the actor is saying, if there really is liquid in the glass from which the actress is drinking. Theatre is illusion, and to pull it off the illusion must be flawless.

Stage managing is a paradox of unseen effort. An audience should never know how hard you've worked, or even that you exist at all. Don't take reviews too seriously, but if they say, "aside from some rough technical cues" or "when the set changes get smoother," you may not be doing an adequate job. To be unmentioned is a stage manager's best review.

Train your crew to be calm so that they don't draw extra attention to a problem in an emergency. If you or the crew members act as though you belong on stage, sweeping up the broken glass or resetting the fallen picture, the audience will probably think you do. Think invisible and even if you aren't, you will be less distracting. Don't race through the lobby or bang stage doors. Stay calm, keep your voice low, and make as little fuss as you can. Instruct your crew to do the same, if they don't already know. Theatre people, with their inevitable flair for the dramatic, frequently overreact to unexpected technical problems. Solve them quietly and keep the show on track.

One of a stage manager's countless responsibilities is to rehearse actors for replacement parts. This is one reason the prompt script must be kept up to date even after the show is running. The new actor should watch the show to get a feel for it, then go over the blocking with the stage manager, work with the choreographer and music director, and, finally, run scenes with the cast.

This assumes you have advance notice. In an emergency, forget everything but getting the blocking and choreography. Actors can carry a script if necessary. The best approach to a fast replacement is being calm and imparting that calm, and confidence, to the actor. The fewer people giving directions, the better. He needs to relax into the role; he'll have plenty of adrenaline to keep him on his toes as it is, so the more composed you stay, the better chance he has of learning what's necessary to carry on quickly. Don't try to teach the whole show all at once if the part is big and time is too limited. Work a scene at a time or an act at a time so that it can be assimilated more easily. But most important, be calm and instill confidence.

From the routine to the unexpected, take pride in every aspect of your job. Whether you are sweeping the stage or calling the show in the midst of crisis, do the absolute best you can. You will be a tremendous asset to any theatre.

·⟦ 4 ⟧·

Authority

[*The difficulties of the stage manager at rehearsal, depend to a great extent on the members of the company. If they are captious,
obstinate, or incapable, he must learn to be
patient and do his best with the art of persua-
sion. Amateurs cannot be driven for they are
perfectly independent; nor do they realize that
the authority of the stage manager is, or
should be, absolute. On the professional stage
the stage manager not infrequently abuses his
position and becomes a bully. . . . Now this
sort of treatment would simply break up the
company, nor indeed is it necessary that they
(or professionals either) should be subjected
to it.*]

STAGE managing is an imposing responsibility. The show
lies in the stage manager's hands. You start it, keep it going,
and, in disaster, may have to stop it. The entire company,

from the star to the grips, depends on you. Do not get caught up in all that power. As one of the most authoritative people in a production, the stage manager sets the tone. Creating an atmosphere of respect benefits the show in countless ways.

Giving orders is the stage manager's responsibility. How this is done can make life easy or miserable for everyone. It is tempting to become a tyrant when people are looking to you for direction. A good stage manager not only knows how to run a show but does so in an aura of respect and courtesy. Manage by supporting instead of demanding. Use your power to serve. Use it to make the production better, rather than feeding your own ego.

Authority with a light touch is more efficient. After all, people do theatre because they want to, not because they have to, which in itself implies cooperation. For example, saying "please" and "thank you" generates a pleasant atmosphere (as in "Places, please" and *"Quiet!* Thank you"). Accept that people may not like what you have to say, but say it politely and they will respond positively. Ask crew members or an assistant stage manager to get something for you rather than demanding it: "Could you please bring me the . . . ?" instead of "Bring me the . . ."

When you are new to stage management, older or more experienced people may intimidate you. A student who stage manages a professor can feel pretty awkward. It is important to have the confidence to exert your authority. Your confidence grows out of your thorough understanding of the production. You may not have experience, but if you know the show and what you are supposed to do, you will be in a stronger position.

Your voice is a tremendous asset. Speak loud enough to

be heard, but don't shout or sound hostile. Yelling and pro-
jecting are vastly different. When giving notes to the company, be certain that what you are saying deserves to be
heard. Decide exactly what you want to say. Be concise. If
you need notes to remember things, use them. Get people's
attention as politely as possible and make sure you have it
before you start talking. Speak clearly. Use eye contact. Be
friendly. And don't forget to say "thank you" when you are
finished. Thank people for listening and for following your
instructions or fulfilling your requests. Presumed cooperation works. Chances are that when they are approached in
this manner, people will do as you ask.

Respect your colleagues by withholding cryptic comments or uninvited opinions. Restraint is one of the most
vital points of theatre etiquette. Typical comments that
upset people are, "Is that really what we're going to use?"
"These aren't the lights, are they?" "That dress is so gross,"
and, everybody's favorite, "This doesn't work." This last re-
mark is not always unwarranted, but because it is so frequently thrown about, the usual response is, "Yes, it does,
you just don't know what you're doing." Work with the ob-
ject and use it first before you disclaim it.

The excitement of being part of a show attracts people
to a competitive, consuming, and in most cases financially
unrewarding career. People do theatre because they love it,
which is why they put so many resources and so much energy into it. But passion also makes us more vulnerable to
criticism. It is easy to take remarks personally when you've
put yourself on the line so completely. Being aware of another person's feelings helps to avoid some of the inevitable
ego bruising. Everyone should have the freedom to make
mistakes and try new ideas without any dampening atti-

tudes ("You can't do that, it will spoil my design"). If their concept is given a chance, it might enhance your design.

There is room for constructive criticism, but some criticism handed out in rehearsals and production meetings does not serve to improve the show; it only bolsters your ego at the expense of another's.

At times you will have to set aside your preferences and forgo having your own way in order to do what's best for the production. Sometimes that means changing your style by exerting more or less control. For instance, I never like to call entrance warnings for cast members because I feel that actors should be responsible for their own entrances. But I once worked for an opera company in which the chorus wouldn't move from backstage unless they were called. When the director told me, "That's the way it's always been," and implied, "and the way it always will be," I called the entrance warnings. Better to get the chorus on stage than try to prove a point. Be flexible with different companies and their inevitably different styles.

Stage management takes an enormous amount of strength and effort. With that potent sensation comes the humbling knowledge that if you blow it, everyone goes down with you. The paradox of stage managing is using the strength it takes to run a show to satisfy the needs of the show. Lead by serving. Understanding that paradox is a never-ending challenge and can be an immensely rewarding journey.

Set an example for the company. Be on time. Be prepared. Do the less pleasant parts of your job without complaint. Listen to the complaints of others and respond to them in positive ways (as opposed to feeding their negativity). Keep the morale up, especially during difficult times such as technical rehearsals or emergency cast replacements. This is what it means to "lead by serving." Put the company's needs before your own and you will gain the respect from company members that manifests itself in your authority.

·⟦ 5 ⟧·

Safety

ALTHOUGH it may not be included as part of a job description for stage managing, being responsible for safety issues is paramount. Theatres can be dangerous areas in which high-risk activities take place. During rehearsals, dancers and performers who are not concerned with the potential hazards work amidst power tools and building materials. In performance, walls fly in and out, staircases and platforms glide across the stage, actors climb all over set pieces and leap from heights. To increase the danger, much of this happens in dim lights or blackouts.

It is everyone's responsibility to be careful, but the stage manager must be particularly aware of keeping the stage and backstage safe. Keep the backstage area clean. Once the show has opened, clear out tools, paint, or other clutter that collects during tech week. Even during tech rehearsals, pick up as much debris as possible; store it in the shop, or at least out of the traffic pattern. Keep ladders, cables, or extra lighting instruments well away from the playing area. Once the lights are set, tape down all cables with duct tape. If anyone will be walking over the cables, cover them with carpet remnants and tape that down securely as well. Make sure the cords from running lights are taped down or out of the way.

Sweeping the stage is an act of caution as well as cleanliness. Loose nails or screws are deadly, and sweeping brings to your attention any problems with the stage surface. Allow no one backstage without shoes. If actors are required to be barefoot while on stage, they should wear shoes to their entrance and have them available at their exit.

When you check the preset, always examine furniture for wobbly table or chair legs, especially if the furniture is used for other than its intended purpose. Inspect the rigging of the flying pieces. Confirm that the work lights are operating. Always keep spare bulbs at your work station. Use glow tape to delineate furniture, stairs, or doors during blackouts.

Working fire extinguishers are a must backstage. Know how to use them. Teach the tech director, crew, and assistant stage managers how to use them as well. If the theatre has a fire curtain, learn how to operate it.

Safety requires the repeated warnings of rules so basic that everyone should know them. You'll know you are doing your job if you feel like the class monitor. Remind the cast (as often as necessary) "NO RUNNING BACKSTAGE." In shows with children, "Walk, DON'T RUN!" should be your mantra. Occasionally exits are followed closely by an entrance from another part of the set, or quick changes require a dash to or from the changing booth. If running is absolutely necessary, keep the paths cleared of people and things.

Provide adequate light. This cannot be emphasized

enough. Have the cast rehearse entrances and exits on the set in full light before they practice them in the dark. Once you start rehearsing in dim light, position people with flashlights at dangerous exits. Aim the light at the floor, away from audience sight lines. There should be just enough light to help orient the actor. Be prepared to guide actors offstage who are blinded by the sudden shift between stage lights and blackouts. Until you've experienced it, it is impossible to conceive how hard it is to readjust to darkness after the brilliant lights.

Actors may be called upon to do difficult, dangerous stunts. As stage manager, you can contribute to their safety. Maintain an atmosphere backstage that discourages fooling around. If the cast and crew know you take safety seriously, they will be more likely to as well.

Beyond these precautions, arm yourself with a good first-aid kit and access to a phone. You may never have to call a fire truck or an ambulance, but you can never afford to be complacent. A friend of mine stage managed a show where paramedics were called three times on opening night. Anything can happen.

The ability to keep your head while those about you are losing theirs is a priceless asset. Accidents happen in spite of every precaution. Staying calm and helping others to be calm is the most effective response in an emergency. Theatre people are a high-strung bunch. The nervous energy on an opening night could power the Empire State Building; imagine the voltage generated in a crisis. Hyper-emotion is contagious. So is being collected. Speaking in a low quiet voice and physically touching people helps calm hysteria. Learn a few basic relaxation techniques, as well as first aid and CPR.

Safety is not one of the more glamorous aspects of a stage manager's job, but it is one of the most important. You are protecting yourself and others from accidents and injuries when you are careful and make certain the work surroundings are safe.

∘⟦ 6 ⟧∘

Variations on the Job

DEFINING a stage manager's job too specifically is a futile exercise, because in virtually every theatre it will be different.

The physical aspects of the theatre will make a difference. Is it a big theatre? A small one? Does it have a proscenium stage, or a thrust, or is it in the round? Are you performing outside, or touring to different locations? Are you rehearsing in several different places? Are you rehearsing one show while performing another?

If the theatre is quite large you will have to get used to the physical space: the time it takes to get from the light booth to backstage or from the dressing rooms to on stage. Quick-change booths may be more necessary; in a small theatre the dressing rooms may be so close to the stage that they can be used for quick changes. The size of the theatre impacts the number of dressing rooms and prop areas. A big theatre may have quite a bit of storage space backstage. A small theatre will require more organization in storing set pieces off stage.

If the theatre has a proscenium stage, it will probably have a grand drape and perhaps a fire curtain. Sets can be preset and changed behind the curtain. On a thrust stage, which extends out into the audience area, or a theatre in the round, where the audience surrounds the stage, presets will have to be done before the house opens, and scene changes will be done in view of the audience. That may require costuming the crew.

If you are performing in an outdoor venue, you will need weather contingency plans. You may have little or no backstage area. You may not have power for headsets. Props and costumes will require protected storage between performances, and you will need to have tools available for repairs since you won't be near a scene shop.

If you are taking a show on the road, organization is critical. You can't count on theatres or spaces in which you are performing to have everything you need. You will have to strike and pack up the show after every stop, as well as loading it in at each new location. The theatres you visit may be very different sizes, so adjustments to the set or blocking may be necessary. Rehearsing in several locations takes almost (but not quite) the organizational skills of taking a show on the road. You must make sure the performers for each rehearsal know where it is. Rehearsal props and furniture will have to be hauled from place to place.

If you are rehearsing one show while performing another, you may have to pack and unpack props, costumes, and set pieces before and after rehearsals. You will also have to stay focused on the show you are running while immersed in the deadlines and stresses of rehearsals. You may also have to share performance or rehearsal space with another company, which will demand even more coordination of time and space.

You may not even be in a location created for theatre. Parks, street corners, warehouses, church sanctuaries, prisons, and school cafeterias have all been utilized as performance spaces. Theatre can be and is done absolutely anywhere, and the setting definitely affects the stage manager's responsibilities.

There are also countless different types of theatre, from nonmusical dramas or comedies, to musicals, contemporary performance art, the classics, revues, dance productions, or opera. If you know how to read music, you can stage manage opera or dance productions. Opera is especially exciting since it often has grandiose sets, special effects, and is performed in a foreign language. Following a musical score calls for extra concentration; you can't as readily find your place in music as you can listening to lines. It may help to get a tape of the score to familiarize yourself with the music, since you may not attend rehearsals until you move on stage. (Often that's the case with opera; an assistant director takes the blocking, and there is no need to have someone on book.) Calling a show to music is just one more way to experience a different aspect of stage managing.

The number of people involved will affect your job. If you have an assistant director, assistant stage manager, or production manager, your responsibilities change. You may fill all of those positions yourself, or you may have all kinds of help. A production manager may run auditions, print and distribute rehearsal schedules, arrange photo calls, and recruit crews. An assistant stage manager may give the time calls, check the sign-in sheet, preset scenes, or even run some rehearsals. If these positions are not filled for a production, you'll have to do those things. It's a good idea to clarify your specific duties before you get involved with a company or production.

A fundamental part of stage managing is calling light cues. But if the lighting operator takes his own cues while you run the show backstage, your approach to running the show will be totally different than it would be if you were tied to the script. You may act as set crew chief, prop runner, or occasionally as dresser, but be sure to function as the stage manager during rehearsals: taking blocking, following book for lines, running rehearsal props, and taking notes.

The stage manager may operate the grand drape or the houselights, or he may cue someone else to do those jobs. The stage manager may cue the crew directly, or cue an assistant stage manager who then cues the crew. You may operate slides or ring doorbells or phones. Being involved in the actual operations (as opposed to cueing others to do them) requires extra vigilance to stay with the big picture. It is easy to fail to stay with the prompt script if you are doing actions instead of cueing them.

Theatre is a fulfilling activity in part because of the divergent groups of people it brings together in a close and intimate setting. You work with an endless spectrum of individuals, all in it for different reasons, coming from different backgrounds, and going off in different directions. And frequently you do it for free, or virtually no pay. Of course, even that varies within a company. It is important not to make salary distinctions—everyone is vital to the production, and money can't be used as a definition of worth. We are all there to do good theatre.

Because so much theatre is done gratis by participants, consider the needs of volunteers. Even if you are getting paid, you may work with people who are not. Here are some suggestions: Don't waste volunteers' time. Know what you want them to do and get them involved right away. Otherwise they'll just drift away and probably not drift back. Pay attention to other people's ideas; they may be better than your own. They may also be useless, but don't dismiss them outright on the grounds that the person suggesting them is not "professional." Being professional has nothing to do with a paycheck and everything to do with attitude. It is doing the best you can, taking pride in your work, and working for the good of the whole production. Express gratitude to volunteers, sincerely, over and above the usual "please" and "thank you." You must make moving a piece of scenery a worthwhile experience so that the person who moved it will come back and move it again. Let volunteers know how important they are to the show as a whole. "We couldn't do it without you" is rarely an inappropriate phrase. Hearing "Thank you, you did a great job" stayed with me a lot longer than any of the salaries I earned.

Theatre has so much about it that is gratifying: the joy of listening to an audience's reactions, the excitement of watching visions and ideas made real, the warmth and camaraderie of working together with others for a common goal—the creation of characters, ideas, worlds. However you do it, wherever you do it, it will be new, different, and, hopefully, special every time. Stage managing can and probably will spill into the rest of your life. The skills you use to run a show will stay with you forever.

⁘ 7 ⁘

Challenges of
Theatre Life

THEATRE presents endless challenges, personal as well as professional. It gives you never-ending opportunities to grow as an individual as well as a stage manager.

Being committed to theatre means subscribing to the theory that "the show must go on." It means being willing to put theatre before every other part of your life. It is a *huge* requirement, and one that separates the serious from the dilettantes. A major frustration in working with community groups is a lack of commitment: too many lame excuses for absences. Don't do theatre unless you are willing to give it your all. And don't stage manage unless you are willing to be present from beginning to end every time there is an audition, rehearsal, production meeting, photo call, or performance. Depending on the theatre, you may not have to attend all these events, but you need to be willing to if called upon.

Theatre is a way of life as well as a job. Expect to miss holidays with your family, class reunions, friends' weddings, and other personal events. The hours alone isolate you from the rest of society. If you do it while supporting yourself with another job, all your evenings and weekends will be consumed. If you do it full time to support yourself, you will probably work from noon to midnight Tuesday through Sunday. And, like as not, you'll be rehearsing or doing extra shows on holidays. But the cast and the crew are your family, so special occasions are always acknowledged, and there's no lack of festivities and celebrations.

Theatre requires a great deal of self-discipline. Opening night is the deadline. Ready or not, the show goes on. But no one makes you do your work on time. Nothing keeps you from waiting until the last minute to get the job done. Some creative people claim to work best under pressure; they say that waiting until the last minute is the catalyst they need to be creative. (Many of these people are insecure and use that as an excuse to avoid presenting their work for possible rejection.) You will work with any number of these tiresome procrastinators. Learn to accept them and do not let them drive you crazy. If you find yourself always running late, then panicking to get things done, reconsider your own work habits. Use all the time you have and get the job done as early as you can. You may stop procrastinating when you realize how much better your work is when you don't put it off. After you get organized, you can approach the next challenge: boredom.

Running seven performances a week for eight to ten weeks can make the most complicated show routine. As a way of keeping shows fresh, give each production a specific goal. A goal could be as simple as "I will be five minutes early at every rehearsal" or as difficult as "I will memorize the set elements in each scene so that shifts run more efficiently." Consider learning to operate the light board or sound equipment. Working with a particularly difficult actor gives you the opportunity to hone your "people" skills—keeping him happy while keeping the rest of the cast from killing him. There may be an opportunity to stand in for cast members at rehearsal. Reading lines while taking blocking (and being able to take blocking from the stage instead of from your usual rehearsal spot) can be a real challenge. Find out if the director wants you to run line rehearsals or the choreographer would like you to run dance rehearsals to review numbers that need polishing.

The rewards of taking on new responsibilities are countless and will give you skills that will serve you in theatre and out of it. New skills will help you do your job more effectively and can make your theatrical life easier. Look at the areas of stage managing you like least and try to find some approach that makes them more fun. Anticipate some of the traps, the quicksand that drags you down when you least expect it. The challenges are never-ending. Every production, every performance is unique. The opportunities to learn are infinite.

•⟦ 8 ⟧•

Other Theatre Jobs

MOST people enjoy or are more adept at one or two areas in theatre, but those specialties can be enriched when one understands what other people do as well. Experience in one area enhances skills and knowledge in others. Consider working in various areas to make yourself more flexible for the job market as well as a better stage manager. Here is a quick review of some other areas.

Props

There are two distinct parts to the properties job: producing the props, and running the properties part of the show. The same person may or may not do both jobs. If you are responsible for producing the props, there are three ways to obtain those that the theatre does not already have: building, borrowing, or buying. The more realistic and contemporary the show, the more likely you are to buy or borrow; the less realistic or older the period, the more likely that you will build them.

The prop plot may change once rehearsals start (when

the director decides that the only way to save a scene is to give everyone something to play with), but if you organize early the changes will be easier to manage. If you read the script and it calls for a dozen telephones for the chorus to dance with—*Cabaret* comes to mind immediately—do not delay the inevitable: call other theatres, or if you are reduced to building, get to work figuring out how to attach the little hang-up hook on the side so it will be actor-proof. Props don't go away if you ignore them. The more time you have to look for a vacuum cleaner that chases the maid around the stage, or sixteen working ukeleles, the better off you are (not to mention giving the sixteen gentlemen who must learn to play "I Want to Be Happy" a little extra time). Face reality: talk to the director, find out what he or she wants, what the budget is, and how many miracles you will have to perform.

Success in borrowing props is based on technique—say "please" and "thank you," take good care of things, and return them promptly when you have finished with them. Consider letting actors know how much a borrowed prop is worth by leaving the price tag on during rehearsals. Remind the cast as often as necessary not to play with the props, not even to *touch* anything that their character does not use.

Be realistic. Do not borrow priceless antiques for heavy action scenes. If a teacup gets slammed down fifty-six times in the run of a show, don't use china that can't take that kind of abuse. Common sense prevents many nightmares. Every theatre person has stories to tell about a chandelier that came crashing down because it wasn't rigged correctly, or a sixty-year-old brass cash register that was knocked off a countertop by a drop that was flown in too hastily. Disasters are the stuff of show biz—and it doesn't pay to think, "That'll never happen to me." Anything that *can* happen, *will* happen.

Actors are the ones who have to use the props, so accommodate their wishes whenever possible. This is especially true when it comes to food on stage. Eating during a show can be one of the most difficult things an actor has to do, particularly since stage food is rarely well prepared. Cold food is bound to turn warm, and hot food turns cold. Sometimes facsimiles are served—for example, cottage cheese with yellow food coloring for scrambled eggs. For a performer to concentrate on the action and deliver lines while chewing and swallowing unappetizing food strikes me as beyond the call of duty. Take mercy on the poor artist and ask her what she would like. Discuss how you can make it more palatable. Does she want watered-down grape juice or cranberry juice for the wine? Sugar in the iced tea that's supposed to be whiskey? At the very least, warn her of what to expect. For *How the Other Half Loves* I didn't want to use real chicken noodle soup since the actress has to throw the soup at an actor, so someone suggested I use cut-up shoelaces and water. The poor actress spent half the scene chewing the shoelace. Thank goodness she didn't try to swallow it!

Food can be dangerous if not treated with respect. Be certain you are never serving anything that has spoiled. Store it where it will be safe from insect life between shows. Once, in *The Odd Couple*, Felix was showing his burnt steak to Oscar and the Pigeon sisters when a large cockroach crawled out from under the meat. The Pigeons' cries of sympathy were certainly convincing that night. Wash dishes after every show and make sure they are clean before and during rehearsals. Never serve anything you wouldn't want to eat yourself.

Follow the Golden Rule: do to others what you would have done to you—be considerate. It will pay off tenfold. Actors will look forward to working with you, sing your praises to all who will listen, and maybe even recommend you for a job. And all because you took the time to make sure the coffee they had to drink on stage was still warm.

Costumes

My first professional job backstage was as a dresser for *The Owl and the Pussycat,* which is a two-person show that has at least nine quick changes for each actor—many of them simultaneous. When the director interviewed me he asked, "Do you have any experience dressing?" I thought, "Sure, I've been doing it since I was two," and I said, "Oh yes." I had no idea what I was getting into. I knew nothing about the intricacies of a quick change: how to preset costumes or work with the actor to complete a change of clothes in thirty seconds. Fortunately the actor and actress in the show were patient and helpful when they realized I was inexperienced but a quick study. As a dresser, I enjoyed assisting the performers and the sense of teamwork that developed.

It is as necessary for dressers and actors to rehearse together as it is for the actors to rehearse with one another. The dresser must consider ahead of time how to preset the costumes; how to lay them out in the change booth so that each piece is available in the order in which it is needed. The change area needs a mirror, makeup, and a comb or brush. There may not be time for major repairs, but safety pins and some kind of tape must be available. If it is a *really* quick change, the stage manager can time the dresser and actor with a stopwatch to make sure the change can be accomplished in the allotted time.

The best attribute for a dresser is the ability to be calm. You can move faster if you aren't flustered. You also help the actor stay in control if you don't contract their nervousness. For especially high-strung actors, or ones who have problems with their lines, be prepared to give them the opening line of their next scene before they leave the change booth.

The wardrobe person is responsible for keeping the costumes clean and in good repair. Doing the laundry and hauling costumes to and from the dry cleaners is a thankless job. Enlist the cast's help as much as you can. Request that the actors put their costumes in the appropriate piles for laundry and dry cleaning, with the pockets empty and jewelry removed. If the costume isn't in the pile, it doesn't get cleaned. Whenever the costumes are cleaned, tell the actors to check their costumes *as soon* as they get to the theatre. Don't let them wait until they are due on stage to find out that the cleaner has lost a scarf or shrunk a dress.

Acting

Performing was a small but not insignificant part of my career. I took the required acting classes in college and decided that baring my soul to strangers in order to get in touch with the character was not my idea of a good time. The pinnacle of my acting career was doing the gorilla in *Cabaret*. (I stage managed the production and was undoubtedly cast for the part to save a salary. I was also the only person who auditioned. I wanted the part so much that I agreed to make my own costume.) As a dancing gorilla dressed in a tutu, wearing a hat with a bouncing flower, I was a sure hit. But my favorite part was calling "places" for Act II in my gorilla suit.

Being on the performers' side of the set enabled me to empathize with the actors. When the mylar rain curtain, which was our backdrop, came down one night, I learned how distracting set problems can be. When my fellow performer changed the words to a song, I had to decide whether to stick to the choreography or adjust it to accommodate the new order of verses he was singing. The whole experience certainly added to my respect and admiration for performers.

Lights

Being a lighting operator tested my nerves more than any other job. When the lighting operator makes a mistake, the whole audience sees it. But lighting was important for me because it helped my cue calling as a stage manager. I learned about the reaction time from hearing "Go" to moving the dimmer, and the lag time from moving the dimmer to seeing the light change. I also experienced the pressure of fast changes and multiple demands that the lighting operator must tolerate during technical rehearsals, which made me more patient as a stage manager. Some lighting designers build their cues during rehearsals, which means the operator is constantly having to make adjustments and write in new cues.

Other Essential Jobs

I worked box office in several different theatres, and house managed in one. After being a house manager, I became more tolerant of late curtain times.

In college I was exposed to carpentry and painting, but I never developed further interest. Still, I can read ground plans well enough to tape out the stage for rehearsals, and I can do emergency set repair. Building props gave me plenty of time in the shop to learn basic construction techniques, such as which tools do what job best.

As for running the show as a grip, I did more than enough of that (as my back will attest). And even if I never worked on a fly crew, I certainly pulled lines thousands of times to open and close grand drapes or raise and lower roll drops. Much of my ability to organize and choreograph set changes came from finding out as a grip what didn't work.

All of these experiences helped me as a stage manager. They gave me new perspectives and more confidence. I learned to appreciate a costumer's need for plenty of time for fitting with the actors. I learned to tolerate the seemingly endless time it took to set the right lighting cue. I learned patience with the house staff in their efforts to deal with latecomers.

Each aspect of a production has its own expertise. Building and painting scenery, cabling sound equipment and monitors, assisting fast costume changes, hanging and focusing lights, moving scenery, setting wigs or hairdos, applying makeup, creating props, designing a dress that makes a frumpy person look elegant (or vice versa)—*all* is magic, from the most tedious task to the grandest. No one does it alone. Respecting the responsibilities and challenges of everyone in the production makes you more effective. Knowing how to do other jobs can actually be the salvation of a show in a crunch.

Appendices

I. Glossary

blocking - The movements actors make on stage, spelled out by the director in rehearsals. The stage manager writes the blocking in his or her prompt script.

call - (1) The time you are due at the theatre. (2) Warnings given by the stage manager to tell the company how long before the show starts (usually half-hour, fifteen, five, and places). (3) The stage manager telling the lightboard operator or the grips when their cue is (as in "calling cues").

callboard - A large bulletin board where notices of importance to the production, such as the company rules, rehearsal schedule, costume-fitting schedule, and sign-in sheet, are posted.

costume plot - A list of all the costume pieces in the show, organized either by scene (with each performer's costumes noted) or by performer (with their costumes listed by scene).

cue - (1) The moment at which something needs to happen—for example, a light cue, when the lighting instruments are to change; or a cue line—the end of the previous line when an actor is to speak. (2) A particular setting of the lighting instruments for a scene (the lighting designer and director may look at a cue during tech rehearsal).

deck - Backstage area immediately off the set on the floor. For example, the deck is where the platforms are stored between scenes; the deck crew moves the platforms.

downstage - The part of the stage closest to the audience.

dresser - The person who assists the actors with quick costume changes and general wardrobe needs.

drop - A large piece of painted canvas hung from a pipe, which can be rolled up and down or flown in and out, used as background for a scene.

flat - Wooden frames covered with painted muslin to form walls for a set.

fly - Bringing scenery hung on pipes on stage or off stage with the use of ropes.

french scenes - Scenes defined by characters' entrances and exits rather than changes in time or place.

grip - Person who moves the scenery during the production.

ground plan - Drawings of the layout of the set(s) as seen from above.

house - The area in a theatre where the audience sits.

in/out - "In" refers to something being on the stage, "out" is off stage.

in 1, in 2 - In 1 is the area just upstage of the first tormentor; in 2 is the area just upstage of the second tormentor, and so forth. These terms are used to specify entrances for actors or scenery.

light booth - The room where the lighting operator works the lights, usually located above the audience in the back of the house. The stage manager may also call the show from there.

light plot - A list of light cues in the show, with details of which dimmers (a group of instruments plugged together) are increased or decreased and by how much, each time any lighting instrument changes. There is also a light plot that indicates where the instruments are hung and into which circuits they are plugged.

load-in - Moving the set into the theatre.

model - A small creation of the set to scale, which shows what the set will look like when built.

on book / off book - "On book" refers to the actors using their scripts to read their lines in rehearsal. "Off book" means they must have the lines memorized and cannot refer to their scripts.

preset - Placement of props, costumes, set pieces, or lights before a scene.

prompt script (or prompt book) - The stage manager's script, which has blocking and light, sound, and set-change cues and warnings written into it.

properties or props - Objects used in the production by the actors. Set prop or set dressing refers to objects that help create the scene but that actors do not use.

properties plot - A list of each prop and its location for each scene.

proscenium arch - The stage opening which forms the frame for an imaginary wall between the stage and the audience.

read-through - The rehearsal (usually the very first rehearsal) at which the play is read by the cast, who usually sit at a table rather than walk around.

rehearsal props - Props used specifically at rehearsals, often just a representation of the real prop (for example, a stick for a sword or a paper cup for a glass).

running crew - The people who set up and move the props or scenery during performances.

scrim - A backdrop made of fabric that can be opaque when lit from the front and translucent when lit from behind.

set changes or scene changes - Rearranging the set pieces between each scene to create the next setting.

shift or scene-change plot - A list of the location of each set piece, scene by scene, who moves each one, and where it is moved in order to create the next scene. *Alfresco* refers to a scene change taking place in view of the audience, which may require costuming the crew or running special light cues.

shinbuster - A lighting instrument placed approximately at shin level.

sign-in sheet - A spreadsheet that lists all the performers and the dates of each performance, so that each actor may check off the appropriate box indicating he or she is present at the theatre for the performance or rehearsal. The stage manager can then easily see if the entire cast is at the theatre.

stage left/stage right - The actors' right or left, as they face the audience. House left and house right refer to the audience's left and right.

strike - To remove props or set pieces from a scene, or tear down the entire set.

teaser - A short black curtain hung above the stage area that masks the lighting pipes and instruments.

technical rehearsals - Rehearsals during which the actors move onto the set and use the actual props. Various types include:

paper tech - The stage manager gets lighting cues from the lighting designer and scene-change cues from the technical director or set designer. The director attends, but the actors do not.

dry tech - It takes place on the set with no actors. All the light cues are run in sequence to view them on the appropriate sets.

cue to cue - The show is run one light cue or set change at a time to see how the cue or set change works, using actors, but cutting (not performing) songs or dialogue between the cues.

full tech - The entire show is run with all parts except costumes and orchestra.

dress rehearsal - All elements are used without an audience. Every effort is made to run the show without stops.

tormentor - A black curtain or flat that is placed at the offstage edge of scenery to mask the backstage area.

traveler - A curtain that opens and closes horizontally across the stage. Can be the "grand drape" (house curtain) or curtains hung upstage as a background to a scene, or hung downstage of part of the set while scenery is moved.

upstage - The part of the stage farthest from the audience.

vamp - A short passage of music that can be repeated to fill time in case of delays in the action.

wagon - A piece of scenery, on casters, on which parts of the set are built.

II. Supplies

General
> flashlights (for yourself and the running crew)
> batteries
> spare bulbs (for work lights and flashlights)
> extension cord
> pencils
> erasers

Tape
> spike (narrow cloth tape in different colors)
> masking
> duct or gaffer
> electrician's
> fluorescent (to put on the edges of steps or set pieces so they are delineated in the dark)
> cellophane

Glue
> super or urethane
> white
> hot glue gun

Tools
> utility knife
> hammer
> Phillips and flat-head screwdrivers
> adjustable wrench or pliers
> screw gun with battery charger

Wardrobe
    safety pins
    needles—at least two threaded, one light, one dark
    shoelaces
    shirt buttons
    bobby pins
    scissors

First aid
    Band-aids, bandages, adhesive tape
    hydrogen peroxide
    ice pack

Whether you are performing in a theatre with a scene shop nearby, or in a park, these items should be readily available backstage. They fit into a medium-size toolbox and are even more important for touring situations or when you are away from the comforts of home.

III. Miscellaneous Tips

Here are everyday hints that I find useful for stage managing. As your own experience accrues, you'll learn many more.

• Spray Scotch Guard on shirt collars before they're worn to help the makeup wash off more easily.

• Store candles in the freezer so they burn slower and drip less (but always use drip guards if people are carrying them).

• Put a piece of blue gel on flashlight lenses and work lights to make them less distracting.

• Run a pencil up and down a slow or stuck metal zipper—the graphite will help make it run more smoothly.

• Watered-down iced tea is typically used for whiskey, ginger ale for champagne, grape juice or food coloring in water for wine. Nothing looks like beer but beer. Make fresh bottles every night, even if they are not drunk on stage. Tea turns moldy very quickly.

• Put water or sand in on-stage ashtrays so that cigarettes will go out completely and not continue to smolder.

• If a cigarette or candle must be lit on stage, always

use wooden stick matches; cardboard match folders are too flimsy. Even if you use a lighter, have wooden matches on the stage as a backup. Place all the matchheads at one end of the box and preset it barely open, with the nonlighting end of one match protruding slightly. Of course, it's always a good laugh when the box is upside down in the cover, and the actor opens it and matches fall all over the floor, but the actor will give you no end of grief (and rightly so).

• Pack real clothes in prop suitcases. The weight will make them look more realistic, and you never know when one might be opened on stage inadvertently.

• Have a backup for plot-turning props in case the real one doesn't work or is not preset. Better safe than sorry. For instance, if you're using blanks in a gun, keep a four-foot 1-by-3-inch board handy backstage for a slap stick. A slightly late bang is better than no bang at all. Put a spare copy of a letter on which the action hinges somewhere on the set.

• If at all possible, have actors and actresses do their own doorbells or knocks. That way everybody knows they will be there when the door is opened.

• It's quieter to speak in a low-pitched voice than a whisper. Whispering is quite sibilant and carries farther.

• Always have a flashlight within hand's reach. Always have spare batteries available for it.

• Always have spare pencils, sharpened and with good erasers.

• Rub a candle along wooden set pieces that rub

against each other when shifted, in order to make them work more easily.

• If a screw has come loose in a piece of wooden scenery, break a wooden match to the depth of the screw hole and insert it as a filler.

IV. Callboard

The callboard is a large bulletin board where important information is posted regarding various aspects of the production, from auditions through closing. It may contain any or all of the following:

1. Audition notices
2. Company policies on complimentary tickets, open or closed rehearsals (whether or not guests are permitted), and other rules
3. Information about publicity photo calls
4. Detailed rehearsal schedules

SAMPLE REHEARSAL SCHEDULES
We used this schedule to produce musical comedies in two weeks while running another musical at night. The actors were expected to know their lines by the first rehearsal, and were frequently involved in both shows.

(No Show in Particular)

Week 1
　　Tuesday 9:00–12:30 Principal choreography
　　　1:30–5:00 Principal music
　　Wednesday 9:00–12:30 Chorus choreography
　　　1:30–5:00 Chorus music

Thursday 9:00–12:30 entire cast, music and choreography

   1:30–5:00 entire cast, music and choreography
Friday 9:00–12:30 entire cast, music and choreography

   1:30–5:00 Block Act I (scenes only, no musical numbers)
Saturday matinee of show in production, no rehearsal
Sunday 12:00–4:00 Block Act II (scenes only, no musical numbers)

Week 2

Tuesday 9:00–12:30 entire cast, music and choreography

   1:30–5:00 Block Act III (scenes only, no musical numbers)
Wednesday 9:00–12:30 entire cast, music and choreography

   1:30–5:00 Run Act I with musical numbers
Thursday 9:00–12:30 entire cast, music and choreography

   1:30–5:00 Run Act II with musical numbers
Friday 9:00–12:30 entire cast, music and choreography

   1:30–5:00 Run Act III with musical numbers
Saturday 9:00–12:00 music and choreography, as needed

   1:00–5:00 Run Show
Sunday 12:00–4:00 Run Show with costumes (no set)
(Sunday after closing performance, strike current show and load-in new one)

Monday 10:00–5:00 Tech rehearsal
7:00 Dress rehearsal
Tuesday 11:00 2nd Dress rehearsal
Tuesday 8:00 Opening night

The following rehearsal schedule for Act 1 of *The Crucible* uses french scenes, which are defined by characters' entrances and exits rather than changes in time or place. Page numbers indicate the part of the script being rehearsed rather than saying Act I, sc. 1, or Act II, sc. 3.

The Crucible

Date	Time	Pages	Cast
Mon., April 6	7:00–8:00	6–9	Paris, Betty, Tituba, Abigail, Susanna
(Blocking)	8:00–9:00	10–15	Paris, Betty, Abigail, Mr. and Mrs. Putnam
	9:00–10:00	19–22	Abigail, John Proctor
Tues., April 7	7:00–8:00	15–19	Abigail, Betty, Mercy, Mary Warren
(Blocking)	8:00–10:00	22–30	Abigail, Paris, Betty, John Proctor, Mr. and Mrs. Putnam, Giles Corey, Rebecca Nurse
Wed., April 8 (Blocking)	7:00–10:00	30–40	Abigail, Paris, Betty, John Proctor, Mr. and Mrs. Putnam, Giles Corey, Rebecca Nurse, Rev. Hale

Thurs., April 9 7:00–10:00 Act I   entire cast for Act I
(Review)

SAMPLE SIGN-IN SHEET
(*No Show in Particular*)

	4/2	4/3	4/4 2pm	4/4 8pm	4/5	4/9	4/10	4/11 2pm	4/11 8pm	4/12
Julie Andrews										
Joel Grey										
Richard Harris										
Mary Martin										
Liza Minelli										
Robert Preston										
Chita Rivera										
Tummy Tune										
Gwen Verdon										

5. Sign-in sheet for the production—a spreadsheet that lists dates of performances and actors' names so they may check in for each performance. List the cast names either in alphabetical order or in order of appearance.

6. Notices of special rehearsals

7. Dressing room assignments

8. Reviews—if a company is willing to post them

SAMPLE MASTER CALENDAR
(No Show in Particular)

1	2 2:00 photo call 10-5 rehearsal	3 10-5 rehearsal	4 4:00 production meeting 10-5 rehearsal	5 9:00 costume fittings 10-5 rehearsal	6 10-5 rehearsal
7 10-3 rehearsal 3-5 costume fittings	8	9 10-5 rehearsal	10 10-5 rehearsal	11 4:00 production meeting 10-5 rehearsal	12 10-5 rehearsal	13 10-5 rehearsal 9-6 load-in
14 10-12 cue to cue tech 1-3 dress parade	15 work on set as needed	16 1-5 orchestra 7pm-12 tech rehearsal	17 1-5 orchestra 7pm-12 tech rehearsal	18 7pm dress reh. with orch.	19 7pm dress reh. with orch.	20 8pm opening
21 2pm matinee 8pm performance	22	23 8pm performance	24 8pm performance	25 8pm performance	26 8pm performance	27 8pm performance
28 2pm matinee 8pm performance	29	30 8pm performance	31 8pm performance			

9. A master calendar for the production, which includes all pertinent dates for the production

V. Sample Shift Plot

42nd Street

When	What	Where	Who
Preset Top of Show	1st electric	IN	
	footlights	U of pit	
	main	IN	
	backstage door unit	DL	
	US traveler	IN	
	piano w/stool	DL	
	tool box	UC	
	flats	USR	
	2 A-frame ladders	USL	
	extension ladder	UC	
	shinbuster plugged in	UC	
	shinbuster plugged in	Off SL	
	shinbuster plugged in	Off SR	
1-1 Backstage	main	OUT	Crew 2
During 1-1-11	mid scrim	IN	Crew 2 and backup
During	shinbuster	DL	Mac
During	shinbuster	DR	Andy
During (1-1-14)	mid scrim	OUT	Crew 2 and backup
During (1-1-14)	middle traveler	IN	Fly-deck
During (1-1-14)	1st electric	OUT	Crew 2
During	shinbuster	Strike	Mac
During	shinbuster	Strike	Andy
During	piano and stool	Strike	Crew 1 or 2?
1-2 Tea Room	flats	Strike	Crew 1 and Crew 2
During	tool box	Strike	Crew 1
During	extension ladder	Strike	Crew 4
During	A-frame ladder	Strike	Crew 2
During (1-1-16)	Gypsy Tea flat	DSL	Crew 3 and Crew 1
During (1-1-16)	table and 5 chairs	DSL	Waiters—Tom and David
During (1-2-19)	Gypsy Tea flat	Strike	Crew 3 and Crew 1
During (1-2-19)	table and 5 chairs	Strike	Waiters—Tom and David
1-3 Backstage	middle traveler	OUT	Fly-deck
	stool	DR	Mac

When	What	Where	Who
1-4 Dorothy's	middle traveler	IN	Fly-deck
	stool	Strike	Abner
	dressing room wagon	DSL	Crew 1 and Crew 2
	chaise	DSL	Crew 3 and Crew 4
1-5 Backstage "Out"	middle traveler	OUT	Fly-deck
	dressing room wagon	Strike	Crew 1 and Crew 2
	chaise	Strike	Crew 3 and Crew 4
1-6 "Dames"	middle traveler	2/3	Crew 2
	2 arches	UC	Crew 4 and Crew 3
	Dames sign	IN	Fly-rail
	2nd legs (masking)	PULL UC	Tom and David
During	hotel room wagon	UR	Crew 1 and Crew 2
During	chaise	UR	Crew 1 and Crew 2
During	Regency Club flat	UL	Crew 3 and Crew 4
During	baby grand	SL	Crew 3 and Crew 4
During	bar	UL	cast
During	small table, 3 chairs	UL	cast
1-7 Regency	middle traveler	OUT	Crew 2
	2 arches	Strike	Crew 3 and Crew 4
	Dames sign	OUT	Fly-rail
	2nd legs	OUT	David and Tom
	adjust piano	DL	Stephanie, Sam, Liz
	adjust bar		Anna, Brittany
1-8 "Pretty Lady"	main	IN	Crew 2
	mid traveler	IN	Crew 1
During	hotel room wagon	Strike	Crew 1 and Crew 2
During	chaise	Strike	Crew 1 and Crew 2
During	Regency Club flat	Strike	Crew 3 and Crew 4
During	baby grand	Strike	Crew 3 and Crew 4
During	bar	Strike	cast
During	small table, 3 chairs	Strike	cast
During	US traveler	OUT	Fly-rail
During	42nd Street signs	IN	Fly-rail
During	main	OUT	Crew 2
During (1-8-47)	mid traveler	OUT	Crew 2
During	mid traveler	IN	Crew 2
During	mid traveler	OUT	Crew 2
During	mid traveler	IN	Crew 2
End of Act	main	IN	Crew 2
Intermission into	arches	prop room	
2-1 Backstage	Gypsy Tea flat	prop room	
	table, 5 chairs	prop room	

When	What	Where	Who
	Regency flat	prop room	
	small table, 3 chairs	prop room	
	grand piano	prop room	
	bar	prop room	
	train station w/panels	UC	
	crate	DL	
	2 ladders (for 2-2)	Center	
	chair (for 2-2)	LC	
	middle traveler	IN	
2-2 "Sunnyside"	main	OUT	Fly-deck
2-3 Out stage door	no change		
2-4 Train Station	ladders and stuff	Strike	cast hands to crew
	middle traveler	OUT	Fly-deck
2-5 Montage	middle traveler	IN	Fly-deck
	help cast off with light	SL & SR	????
2-6 Peggy's Dressing	dressing room	DL	Crew 1 and Crew 2
	chaise	DL	Crew 3 and Crew 4
During	train station panels	Strike	Crew 3 and Crew 4
During	railing	Strike	Crew 1 and Crew 2
During	stairs (4)	Strike	Crew 1, Crew 2, Crew 3
2-7 Train	main	IN	Fly-deck
	middle traveler	OUT	Fly-deck
	dressing room	Strike	Crew 1 and Crew 2
	chaise	strike	Crew 3 and Crew 4
During (2-7-27)	main	OUT	Fly-deck
During	adjust train	UL & UR	Crew 3 and Crew 4
During (2-7-28)	DS scrim	IN	Crew 2
During	train	Strike	Crew 1, Crew 3, Crew 4
During	42nd Street signs	IN	Fly-rail
During	US traveler	OUT	Fly-rail
2-8 Backstage	no change		
Curtain Call	main	IN	Crew 2
	main	OUT	Crew 2

Crew 2 person does travelers and main when Fly person can't

VI. Sample Prop Plot

(*No Show in Particular*)

Act I sc 1
  Preset:
    suitcase L of sofa
    on bar: ice bucket
      tongs
      bottles of gin and vermouth
      pitcher and stirrer
      4 glasses
      ashtray
      matches
    knitting in basket by DL chair
    newspaper and magazines on coffee table
    violin and music on sofa table
  Off SL:
    fish
    gift boxes—one with vase inside
  Off SR:
    tray with coffee pot, sugar, creamer, 4 cups, 4 spoons
    plate of cookies
    telegram and letters
    sheet music
  Personal props:
    notebook and pen in John's suitcoat
    cigarettes and lighter in Mary's purse

During Act I sc 1
take suitcase from John SR

Act I sc 2
Strike:
fish from balcony
empty boxes and wrapping
jacket and tie
violin
Preset:
photo on desk
vase with flowers on mantel
move letters from coffee table to desk

Act II
Strike:
sweep up broken vase
empty ashtray
tray with coffee service from bar
coffee cups from coffee table
Preset:
blanket on sofa
violin on DL chair
Off SL:
suitcase
books

VII. Sample Prompt Script Pages

The following pages are from a prompt script created for *The Elephant Man*, which shows complex light and sound cue sequences as well as blocking. Characters are circled, and the arrows after the sound cues indicate sound up (or on) and sound down (or off).

Warn S 1
House open-
Curtain warmer, gaslights
Warn L 1-4, S 2-4

Preshow-

(W)ent SR X UR X UL stop at pillars to turn up gas lights ex DL

(S)ent with broom SL X UL X D ex UR

S1 ↑ Preshow
L1 (W) at 2nd light
S1 ↓ at (W) ex when complete,
S2↑, L2

The Elephant Man

SCENE 1

HE WILL HAVE 100 GUINEA FEES
BEFORE HE'S FORTY

The London Hospital, Whitechapel Rd. *Enter* GOMM.
Enter TREVES.

(G)ent URXLXD
(T)ent ULXRXD

TREVES. Mr. Carr Gomm? Frederick Treves. Your new lecturer in anatomy. ————————————— S 2 fade ↓

GOMM. Age thirty-one. Books on Scrofula and Applied Surgical Anatomy—I'm happy to see you rising, Mr. Treves. I like to see merit credited, and your industry, accomplishment, and skill all do you credit. Ignore the squalor of Whitechapel, the general dinginess, neglect and poverty without, and you will find a continual medical richesse in the London Hospital. We study and treat the widest range of diseases and disorders, and are certainly ⌐ XL the greatest institution of our kind in the world. ⌐ The Empire provides unparalleled opportunities for our studies, as places cruel to life are the most revealing scientifically. Add to our reputation by going further, and that'll satisfy. You've bought a house?

TREVES. On Wimpole Street.

GOMM. Good. Keep at it, Treves. You'll have an FRS and 100 guinea fees before you're forty. You'll find it an excellent consolation prize.

TREVES. Consolation? I don't know what you mean.

GOMM. I know you don't. You will. (*Exits.*)————— UL , S3 ↑

TREVES⌐ A happy childhood in Dorset. A scientist in an   XL
age of science. In an English age, an Englishman. A
teacher and a doctor at the London. Two books published
by my thirty-first year. ———————— XDR
A house. A wife who loves me, and my god, 100 guinea
fees before I'm forty. Consolation for what? As of the
year AD 1884, I, Freddie Treves, have excessive blessings.
Or so it seems to me. ——————————— XRXU ex UR

Blackout.   L3, S3 ↓, S4 ↑

SCENE 2
ART IS AS NOTHING TO NATURE

Ⓡpull curt. R to L,
⌐ L4, S4 starts ↓

Whitechapel Rd. A storefront. A large advertisement of a ⌐ Man, Woman ent
creature with an elephant's head. ROSS, *his manager.*   ULXDXR on
plat.

ROSS. Tuppence only, step in and see: This side of the grave, John Merrick has no hope nor expectation of relief. In every sense his situation is desperate. ⌐His physical agony is exceeded only by his mental anguish, a despised creature without consolation. Tuppence only, step in and see! To live with his physical hideousness, incapacitating deformities and unremitting pain is trial enough, but to be exposed to the cruelly lacerating expressions of horror and disgust by all who behold him—is even more difficult to bear.   Tuppence only, step in and see!⌐ For in order to survive, Merrick forces himself to suffer these humiliations, I repeat, humiliations, in order to survive, thus he exposes himself to crowds who pay to gape and yawp at this freak of nature, The Elephant Man.

Man ent UR X to others

Warn S5, 6, L5, 5a

Men and Woman XUL and ex

(Enter TREVES *who looks at advertisement)*

ent URXDX to plat.

ROSS. See Mother Nature uncorseted and in malignant rage! Tuppence.

S4 out
XL

TREVES. This sign's absurd. Half-elephant, half-man is not possible. Is he foreign?

ROSS. Right, from Leicester. But noting to fear.

TREVES. I'm at the London across the road. I would be curious to see him if there is some genuine disorder. If he is a mass of papier-maché and paint however—

Ⓡ pull curtain, both ex

ROSS. Then pay me nothing. Enter, sir. Merrick, stand up. Ya bloody donkey, up, up.

S4 ↑

(They go in, then emerge. TREVES *pays.)*

Both ent
S4 ↓

TREVES. I must examine him further at the hospital. Here is my card. I'm Treves. I will have a cab pick him up and return him. My card will gain him admittance.

ROSS. Five bob and he's yours for the day.

Plug in slide proj.

TREVES. I wish to examine him in the interests of science, you see.

ROSS. Sir, I'm Ross. ⌐ I look out for him, get him his living. Found him in Leicester workhouse. His own ma put him there age of three. We—him and I—are in.

Ⓡ bring Ⓣ C

business. He is our capital, see. Go to a bank. Go
anywhere. Want to borrow capital, you pay interest.
Scientists even. He's good value though. You won't find
another like him

TREVES. Fair enough. (*He pays.*) ——————————— Ⓣex UL, S4 ↓

ROSS. Right. Out here, Merrick. Ya bloody donkey, out! —— Ⓑ opens
                                                    curtain S5 ↑, L5

Lights fade out.

SCENE 3

WHO HAS SEEN THE LIKE OF THIS?

TREVES *lectures.* MERRICK *contorts himself to*   Ⓣent UL, L5a,
approximate projected slides of the real Merrick.   screen in,
                                                             S5↓, slide 1

TREVES. The most striking feature about him was his
enormous head. Its circumference was about that of a
man's waist. From the brow there projected a huge bony
mass like a loaf, while from the back of his head hung a
bag of spongy fungeous-looking skin, the surface of which
was comparable to brown cauliflower. On the top of the
skull were a few long lank hairs. The osseous growth on   S6↑
the forehead, at this stage about the size of a tangerine,
almost occluded one eye. From the upper jaw there   ———— slide 2
projected another mass of bone. It protruded from the
mouth like a pink stump, turning the upper lip inside out,   Warn S6↓,7a,
and making the mouth a wide slobbering aperture. The   7b, 8, L6, 7
nose was merely a lump of flesh, only recognizable as a
nose from its position. The deformities rendered the face
utterly incapable of the expression of any emotion———slide 3
whatsoever. The back is horrible because from it hung, as
far down as the middle of the thigh, huge sacklike masses
of flesh covered by the same loathsome cauliflower stain.
The right arm was of enormous size and shapeless. It

suggested but was not elephantiasis, and was overgrown
also with pendant masses of the same cauliflower-like skin.
The right hand was large and clumsy—a fin or paddle   slide 4
rather than a hand. No distinction existed between the
palm and back, the thumb was like a radish, the fingers like
thick tuberous roots. As a limb it was useless. The other
arm was remarkable by contrast. It was not only normal,   slide 5
but was moreover a delicately shaped limb covered with a
fine skin and provided with a beautiful hand which any
woman might have envied. From the chest hung a bag of   slide 6
the same repulsive flesh. It was like a dewlap suspended
from the neck of a lizard. The lower limbs had the
characters of the deformed arm. They were unwieldy,
dropsical-looking, and grossly misshapen. There arose
from the fungous skin growths a very sickening stench
which was hard to tolerate. To add a further burden to his
trouble, the wretched man when a boy developed hip
disease which left him permanently lame, so he could only
walk with a stick. (*To* MERRICK.) Please. (MERRICK   slide BO, S6↓
walks.) He was thus denied all means of escape from his
tormentors.   S7a↑

VOICE. Mr. Treves, you have shown a profound and   unplug projector
unknown disorder to us. You have said when he leaves
here it is for his exhibition again. I do not think it ought to
be permitted. It is a disgrace. It is a pity and a disgrace. It
is an indecency in fact. It may be a danger is ways we do
not know. Something ought to be done about it.
TREVES. I am a doctor. What would you have me do?   Ⓣ XL off plat,
                                       S7b↑ S7a↓
VOICE. Well. I know what to do. I know.   Police ent UL,
                                       S8↑, L6

Silence. A policeman enters as lights fade out.

Index

Actor / Actress, 18–20, 26–30, 49, 51, 53–55, 65–66, 76, 88–89
Assistant stage manager, 61, 64, 75, 80–81

Blackout, 35, 48, 76
Blocking, 34–37, 67–68, 94, 114–118
Book: "on book" and "off book," 34, 35, 37, 57, 96

Cables, 74–75
Call: time due at theatre, 53, 94; as warning of show time, 29,
    56–57, 64, 94. *See also* Cue.
Callboard, 94, 104–108
Choreographer, 33, 39, 50–51
Closing night, 55
Conductor, 32, 46, 50–51
Costume: designer, 31, 49; dresser, 49, 89–90, 95; plot, 17, 94; as
    prop, 23; quick change, 49, 89–90; in rehearsals, 23, 54
Crew, 32, 46–48, 50, 53, 97. *See also* Grip.
Criticism, 50–51, 71
Cue, 94–95; light, 32, 35, 43–44, 58–61, 114–118; shift, 47; sound, 35,
    38, 59, 114–118; standby, 47, 59–60; visual, 47, 59, 61; warning,
    59–60, 114–118
Curtain call, 62

Diplomacy, 27–29, 41, 66, 70–72
Director, 25, 39–41, 44–45, 50–51
Downstage, 36–37, 95
Dresser. *See* Costume.
Dressing rooms, 54, 78, 107

Emergency (how to handle), 67–68, 76

Flashlight (need for), 49, 75–76, 99, 101
Food (as prop), 88–89, 101

Glow tape, 48–49, 99
Grand drape (also called Main), 78, 81, 98, 109–111
Grip, 95. *See also* Crew.
Ground plan, 16, 21–22, 30, 41, 95

Headset, 31, 56, 59–60
House, 57, 95
House lights, 81
House manager, 57, 62, 92

Lighting: board, 32, 60; booth, 61, 95; designer, 30, 43, 50; operator,
    32, 58–60; plot, 96. *See also* Cue.
Load-in, 31, 96

Model, 30, 41, 96
Music director. *See* Conductor.

Notes, 25, 28, 50–51

Opening night, 55
Opera, 80

Places. *See* Call.
Preset, 38, 44, 64–65, 75, 96, 109
Producer, 50
Production meeting, 39
Prompt script / Prompt book, 34–38, 57–59, 96, 114–118
Properties, 96; crew, 32, 53, 65; obtaining, 86–88; plot, 17–19, 38, 96, 112–113; in rehearsals, 16–19, 21, 23–24, 53, 97
Proscenium, 78–79, 96

Quick change. *See* Costume.

Rehearsal: dress, 43; preparing for, 16–23, 42; read-through, 34, 96; schedule, 17, 104–107; technical, 43–45, 54–55, 97–98. *See also* Costume; Properties; Set; Set Change.
Running lights, 56–57. *See also* Work lights.

Scene change. *See* Set change.
Scene plot, 18–20
Script, 16. *See also* Prompt script.
Set, 40, 47, 54; designer, 30, 40, 50; pieces in rehearsal, 16, 18–19, 23. *See also* Set change.
Set change, 46–49, 61 97, 109–111
Shift. *See* Set change.
Sign-in sheet, 56, 97, 107
Sound cue. *See* Cue.
Spike, 48; tape, 99
Stage left / Stage right, 36–37, 97
Standby. *See* Cue.
Strike, 79, 97, 109–111

Taping the stage, 16, 21–22
Teaser, 65, 97
Technical director, 31–32, 39, 44–45, 46–48, 50
Technical rehearsal. *See* Rehearsal, technical.
Tormentor, 65, 98
Traveler, 98, 109–111

Upstage, 36–37, 98

Visual cue. *See* Cue.
Volunteer, 81–82

Wardrobe, 32, 90. *See also* Dresser.
Warning. *See* Cue.
Work lights, 31, 57, 101. *See also* Running lights.

A NOTE ON THE AUTHOR

Linda Apperson has worked in summer stock, dinner theatre, and regional and community theatres in California,
Florida, and Colorado for more than twenty years. Born
in Paxton, Illinois, she made her theatrical debut at the
age of twelve, singing the part of Katisha in *The Mikado*.
She is a graduate of the School of Theatre at Florida State
University, and now works at Stanford University. She
lives in Sunnyvale, California.

CPSIA information can be obtained at www.ICGtesting.com
Printed in the USA
LVOW08s1324170816

500767LV00001B/46/P

9 781566 632010